Pearls

Pearls
(from irritation to beauty)

Roy Mendelsohn

Authors Choice Press
San Jose New York Lincoln Shanghai

Pearls
from irritation to beauty

Authors Choice Press
an imprint of iUniverse.com, Inc.

For information address:
iUniverse.com, Inc.
620 North 48th Street, Suite 201
Lincoln, NE 68504-3467
www.iuniverse.com

ISBN: 0-595-14104-8

Printed in the United States of America

To Arlene

Contents

Preface

The seeds for this book were sown long ago—captured in two events that have stood as symbols to me throughout my adult life. The fact that they both occurred in the same year suggests to me that this was a turning point in my life, and like everything else makes clear that I can only observe what I do; not predetermine it.

The summer after my 10th birthday I approached my annual trip to a sleep away camp with anticipation, a mixture of excitement and anxiety. I loved the camp activities, but my fear of deep water made the time spent at the waterfront difficult. Customarily the first morning was spent taking tests in the water in order to determine eligibility for a variety of recreational options, usually in the evening. On this occasion I noticed a sailboat anchored off to the side and felt a surge of joy at the prospect of being at the helm. Quickly, however, I realized that to have this privilege I had to swim a mile and the children seeking it were already lining up for their turn. Without thinking I found myself joining that group moving closer each moment to the point of diving into deep water.

I had many lessons on swimming, all in shallow water, but my panic at even the idea of being in deep water seemed overwhelming. Finally the point of no return arrived, I took a brief sidelong glance at the sailboat, and somehow flung myself into space. Once I hit the water I realized what I had done, but to my absolute amazement my flailing around was keeping me afloat. These brief moments of awkward effectiveness meant everything, for they gave me the time and panic-free space I needed to surround and gain some mastery over my anxiety. It was a major lesson I was learning about the crippling effects of anxiety itself, and of the importance of facing rather than avoiding it. A vital dimension of the experience concerned my focus on the sailboat; reflecting the powerful attraction of being able to desire something that enhanced my sense of feeling alive.

The second event took place a few months later. It concerned what was an unusual circumstance for me to be in at the time (though quite frequent afterwards). I had apparently ignored a teacher's direction, continuing to be absorbed in my own thoughts, which aroused an intensely angry reaction in her. My usual tendency would have been to feel intimidated by such forceful emotions directed my way, but on this occasion it was quite different. I could see fear in her eyes. The way it came to me then was in an astonished internal realization that she was more frightened of me than I was of her.

From that day forward my entire school experience changed. I could look forward to each day with eager anticipation and enjoy whatever took place without intimidation. I even found myself reacting to "mis-authorities" (those who misuse the positions of power they hold) in ways that often brought unpleasant consequences.

I, of course, have had to learn from my feelings and reactions so they did not just spill out into the world. Whenever unpleasant feelings swell up in me they give me an opportunity to explore their source, and open up areas of darkness. When I can truly learn it results in a whole new way of seeing and experiencing the events in my life.

This book represents the pearls that have emerged from within me. They have come from what I have learned in being open to tracing the source of all the negative feelings I have been confronted with, and from seeking out the part I played in creating them.

Chapter 1

Therapist; One Word or Two?

"How can you possibly sit and listen to peoples' troubles all day long?" This is a question I have been asked on numerous occasions and, since I find it hard to imagine myself doing that, it did get me to thinking about what it was I did. Of course the particular actions I engage in, the words I say, and the understandings I achieve are totally different from one individual to another, but underneath it all there has to be a guiding principle that is basic to how I function in listening to other people

I searched for words to describe clearly just what it was that led my way. It became evident to me that I was always trying to hear from my patients what specifically was required of me for their growth to be facilitated. I listen for a patient's healthy strivings to show or tell me what to say or do, when and how. If I am in tune with their meaning it resonates with the person's deepest yearnings, feels right, and validates the correctness of my understanding. In essence I will have said or done what they have directed.

It can be confusing to define precisely what I mean, for if a patient really knew what was needed to be told or have done, why would my presence be necessary. Clearly it does not mean responding simply to the face value, or openly expressed content, of what is being communicated. Instead it refers to my ability to accurately grasp the implicit, the hidden, and the unknown. With that as a beginning I must then be able to separate it from my own internal reactions and responses, which have been integral to my listening process. Put simply I must be able to be informed by my emotions, not distant or uninvolved; a vital but difficult task indeed and one at which I am not always successful. I would add, however, that when I am not it becomes clear from a patient's reactions.

The process of looking for and discovering validation is vital before I can have any confidence that I am in touch with what is required. In that context, were I to be spending my time listening to a patient's troubles it would be directing attention away from what was most in need of being heard. Such an approach as far as I can see would only serve to feed and strengthen the very things that are wrong.

I recall conducting a seminar in which I expressed these ideas as to how I perceived the therapeutic task. Many of the individuals in the audience, composed of psychoanalysts having various levels of training and experience, were quite disturbed. They felt I was presenting myself as an omnipotent person to be capable of making such distinctions. In the attempt to dispute what I was saying they indicated that they had spent many years in training to learn how the mind functioned and how human beings behaved and thought; as a consequence of which they were in a much better position to determine what it was a patient needed. Furthermore, it was the therapist's responsibility to make this expertise available to a given patient in order to foster his or her growth. Although there was a certain logical sound to these words, to me it seemed (and still does) backwards. I find it hard to conceive of how I, for one, or anyone else, can determine what resides in the depths of another individual's being. We can only listen for them to tell us, and we often make mistakes in understanding what is being communicated. However, the ultimate determiner of the truth or accuracy, regardless of the degree of training or experience that we may possess, as far as I can tell, can only be the individual involved. In my view to think otherwise would be in the direction of omnipotence.

An example of how this appears in a clinical situation was shown in the beginning sessions of a 9 year girl with an early history of sexual abuse. She was removed from her natural family at age two and placed in a foster home where there was a repetition of the abuse. Eventually she was adopted at age 7 by her present family. Her parents were concerned about her inability to form close relationships, her emotional instability and poor control, and an obsession with sexual matters. In addition she didn't do well in school and seemed unreachable.

She came to her first session and insisted that her mother accompany her into my office, behaving as though she was anticipating a battle from me. I simply commented that it looked like she needed to explore this unfamiliar place and didn't feel safe enough without her mother, adding that I would listen for what she had to discover before it was alright for her mother to leave. Her defiant attitude immediately dissolved and she became openly excited at the prospect of her mother joining her, stating that she had been too scared to enter the office alone.

Here I followed her directions to have her mother accompany her, taking them at face value, because I had no idea whatsoever as to what would be best. My listening posture, however, was attuned for any signs that it was a mistake. In this opening moment I went with what was explicit, but did contribute my reading of what may have been behind her insistence. I also specifically called her attention to what I was concerned about, by referring to my search for any indication of feelings within her that she was either unable to communicate or that I might overlook. The change in her attitude appeared to validate my understanding, after which she openly acknowledged that she had been frightened. Thus I was establishing some groundwork for how I would be functioning with her.

She then spent the entire time identifying what she could and could not do in the room. At first she was quite serious, but gradually became teasing and provocative. She asked whether she could destroy different objects that caught her eye or if she could go into my desk, emphasizing that she knew this would be off limits. Although she was blatantly asking for permission to be invasive and destructive, at the same time she was expressing how aware she was of its negative meaning. It suggested that she was informing me of how much she needed me to find some way to provide her with a sense of being contained, held and regulated. By implication things could readily become chaotic and out of control, bringing me the message that I would have to understand her well enough to find a way of interacting so she would not feel destructive. To restrain her physically, or enter those kinds of struggles with her, most likely was what she anticipated at the outset. I thought she might be driven in that direction as a repetition of the very things that had gone awry for her. Thus it was quite a task she was presenting to me and I was attempting to follow it as well as I could.

In the succeeding sessions she was just as adamant that her mother not come in. After making sure that our relationship would be confidential she drew pictures of naked men and women with their bodily products pouring out of every orifice. She was quite explicit in her terminology and took great pleasure in her use of vulgar words. Her attitude towards me in all of this was of expecting me to be delighted in what she was doing. She seemed to see me as a willing recipient of, and participant in, these kinds of experiences, having the aura of sexual overstimulation. Along with it there was a persistent demand for supplies. She clamored for paper, crayons, tape, and food seemingly feeling certain that I would provide them, for it apparently made no difference when I remained silent and didn't comply.

During this period I was gathering information concerning the makeup of her internal world and my listening posture seemed to be taken by her as evidence of my desire to gratify her every wish. A background sense of irritability began to slowly appear so that at one point she fell silent. I told her how I understood what was happening. I thought she needed to see me as being pleased with these images that filled her mind, as well as being ready to gratify all of her wishes, for a reason I didn't as yet understand. It looked like it helped her to feel more confident about herself. While I spoke she looked uneasy, but my words must have reached her in a positive way because she put her head down mumbling something about wanting to feel close to someone. Then very quickly her entire demeanor changed. She began to angrily demand that her requests be granted, as if the moment before had not occurred. When it was apparent to her that I was concentrating upon trying to grasp the meaning of her behavior, she reacted with a concerted effort to attack my belongings, while frantically insisting that these actions had to be permitted.

I thought I had been somewhat off in my understanding of her and she was dramatically bringing this to my attention, which would give me an opportunity to be more accurate. Also I considered the possibility that she was testing my ability to manage things were she to get out of control. Her response to my verbalizing these thoughts was to suddenly shift again. Instead of being a powerful attacker, she looked very soft, vulnerable and uneasy.

My effort to provide her with some understanding of what was either embodied in her approach, or lay behind it, seemed to make a connection, which allowed her to reveal how frightened she was. I simply commented on the rapid change in her feelings and she began to talk, making me believe I was on the right track.

She wanted me to know something important about her early years, glossing quickly over the many incidents of abuse, abandonment, and neglect, and focusing upon what she called her Indian heritage. She felt that she had to keep it alive through her Indian songs and language, making her feel good about herself. Her worry involved an anticipation of my poking fun at this vital part of her. It reminded her of how people in authority had frequently tried to spoil or demean her involvement. In describing the songs and rituals she began to cry, yet was also pleased to see how easily they came rushing into her mind.

My posture, determined by my best reading of what she had been communicating as to what was necessary for her to grow, had seemingly helped her to reach experiences buried within her that reflected a positive and constructive attachment to her past. Apparently the prevalence of deprivation and invasively destructive relationships had made it necessary for her to carefully guard these islands of experience in order to preserve them. They remained relatively inaccessible in the deeper layers of her personality.

The following session occurred months later and showed the changes that were taking place. She entered the office in a playful mood, initiating a reversal of roles by declaring that she was the therapist while addressing me as the patient. Setting the stage she announced that there were really two therapists; one real and good, the other wore a disguise and was evil. The real therapist was understanding, firm, thoughtful, curious and gentle; the evil one was cruel, sadistic, and sexually seductive. The evil therapist tried to act like the good one, but could never successfully accomplish it. Whenever he behaved like the good one he could be exposed simply by provoking him. The real therapist looked for the unspoken meaning of her behavior, reflecting back what he understood, whereas the evil therapist could only respond by attacking in kind. She went on to develop scenarios in which I, as the patient, expressed sexual conflicts. She, in turn, as the therapist, listened and spoke kindly about their deeper meaning. It was in this way that I could know I was in the right place.

Within this role playing game her identification with my therapeutic attitude was apparent, as well as displaying the changes that were occurring. It also gave expression to how I had understood our early interactions, and to how much her provocative behavior was designed to see how sensitive I would be to discovering what she needed within this setting. Another change was noticeable at this time having to do with how she reacted to any lapse of empathy on my part. In the beginning these kinds of failures led to a rapid shift from seeing me as an all gratifying figure to being devastated and driven to attack my person or belongings. Now she could verbalize her perception of a lapse on my part, usually indirectly, and was more contained and introspective. Thus when I was not intune with her she would be reminded of a teacher who did not listen to her.

Whenever I was out of touch with this patient's unspoken or implied messages she saw me as invasive and destructive. By contrast when she felt heard, and thereby safe (and contained), she was able to allow the more vulnerable aspects of herself to surface. Stated simply, an environment was created wherein the healthy and constructive forces existing at the foundation of her personality were sought out and followed. In that sense she was in charge, deeply confident she would not be invaded unless her face value behavior and communications were misunderstood.

There may be times when it is necessary to engage in actions, since words are either not enough, cannot be comprehended, or are completely untrustable. In such a situation it is essential that whatever is done fits what is required to facilitate growth, and that close attention is paid to assess whether that is in fact happening. This means being alert for any evidence of it furthering a therapist's agenda or of resulting from a therapist's inability to find the proper words. The patient's reactions will then serve as an indicator as to whether a therapist has been invasive (the rapist) or empathic to a patient's unconscious messages (therapist).

I was confronted with this dilemma in the treatment of a 6 year old boy referred because his school was concerned about his isolated, withdrawn behavior. His parents, on the other hand, saw him as an independent child, though they did worry about his intense determination to accomplish tasks that were beyond his ability. Nevertheless they were surprised at the depth of the school's concern. He came to the first session looking fearful and embarrassed while clinging to his mother. She was taken aback for he had never exhibited this kind of behavior before. He said that he couldn't talk, but his body could. When I remarked that I would try to understand what his body was saying he immediately left his mother and came into the office.

Here was a vivid moment wherein a child was expressing a piece of internal knowledge. He knew his actions and behavior were communicating things that he couldn't put into words, so that my statement of that being precisely what I would try to understand seemed to offer him some hope. The implication that he then felt safer by leaving his mother tended to validate my view.

Once he entered the first thing he did was to draw a picture calling it his fort. There were no windows or doors so that he was perfectly safe where noone could hurt him. I wondered about the great expense he paid, for it looked as though nothing could come in and he was limited in not being able to get out. Matter of factly he commented that if he wanted to he could find a way out. This 6 year old boy was calling attention to my putting my own meaning into his production, for if I understood him I would know that was not the problem. In correcting me I believe he sensed that I would take it seriously, and in doing so recognize how vital it was for me to respect his autonomy. It was then upon this basis that he agreed to meet with me, as he specifically stated that he thought it was important to see if he wanted to find a way out.

His picture seemed to capture the intense defensive measures he had adopted to leave no opening for anyone to hurt him, while also implicitly indicating how strongly he felt about being in charge. It also showed in all of his movements and behavior. At the same time his attitude tended to verfiy that there was some truth in my words.

His parents, though warm and sensitive, were psychologically naive. They had adopted him when he was 6 months old and had very little information concerning his early life. They only knew he had come from a single parent and his mother had been an extremely disturbed woman who had taken her life after putting him up for adoption. They had been told by the adoption agency that he had suffered some physical abuse at her hands. Subsequently she had become distraught and left the crying baby on their door step. From the parents viewpoint, after an initial period of being quite withdrawn, he had been very responsive to their care. They in fact had been pleased with how he had been developing. His comment about his body talking for him sounded to me like this had some reference to these early events. However, I had no way of knowing how they might be manifested. He did appear responsive and the rapidity with which he was making himself known to me appeared to be a positive sign. I did think that if I was able to establish the proper climate there was a strong possibility he could use the treatment arena to both push against and perhaps enact what was probably unthinkable. Even at this point in time I could imagine myself faced with the prospect of at one and the same time having to make it safe enough to do so, while allowing him the room to express whatever was required in his behavior.

During the early months he vacilliated between laboriously working on some project he had brought in and being teasing and provocative. Slowly he revealed how tightly controlled his emotions were and how fearful he was of "letting go". Someone, including himself, would get hurt. Cautiously he tested me to determine if it was safe. On a few occasions he brought ropes in, jokingly telling me they were to tie me up so I couldn't stop him. He imagined himself being totally in control, as he proceeded to totally ravage and destroy my office. The idea seemed exciting to him.

Shortly afterward he "inadvertently" knocked over objects in the room while talking about people who were weak and helpless and for whom he felt contempt. To me it sounded like a clear message that underneath it all he was seeking to be contained and was worried that I would be unable to provide it in a helpful way. I began by remarking that it looked like he was coming out of his fort and perhaps he feared I wouldn't know what to do, especially when he could knock my things over so easily. His response indicated that I was on the right track, for he laughed, drew a picture of his fort and pointed out the construction work being done on the doors and windows. While he was drawing he made a brief reference to his biological mother for the first time. He imagined being in a distant city where he heard her frantic cries. She was on top of a tall building in total despair preparing to jump. However, he rescued her by stopping her at the very last moment. Clearly he had some knowledge of the circumstances around his early life with his mother. In addition it expressed how dangerous it could be if there was noone there to contain such a destructive act. In his fantasy he was the savior, making it unmistakeable that she had to be stopped. I took this as a direction were this kind of situation to arise between us. My task appeared to be to figure out how to stop him in a way that would enable him to feel helped. He had already shown that if this area of trauma was to be reached the conditions of the treatment had to be safe enough for him to relinquish his rigid defensive armor. Furthermore there were many suggestions that his underlying aggression could be so overwhelming as to be unmanageable. Throughout he had been testing my ability to offer the safety he needed, hinting that he might very well erupt into some out of control behavior. My impression was that he was moving closer to actually attacking me, probably hoping that I could remain steady and not be driven away.

This impression was realized dramatically in a subsequent session. He entered the office appearing wild and uncontrollable; yelling, racing around the room, and suddenly grabbed an object and threw it against the wall. I held him gently as he screamed out in rage, "Don't trap me. You're hurting my feelings!". I released him only to have him repeat his wild behavior. This time when I held him I told him that he had the key to get free, identifying it as simply telling me to let go. He continued the same behavior, I held him, he gave me the signal to let go, and he was freed. This went on uninterruptedly for a considerable period of time until with great surprise he exclaimed, "I'm playing". This had never happened to him before and he went on to describe his inability to pretend in many situations. Although he could imagine things he hadn't known how to play, since whenever he put what was happening in his mind into action everything built up and he ended up being driven by an uncontrollable force. He lost all sense of what was taking place and didn't know how to stop what had now become an explosive outburst.

It was striking to hear him finding words for what had previously been unthinkable. The out of control attack was at first accompanied by rage, alternating with a fear of being enveloped. When the control of my actions was placed in his hands (the key) it became possible for him to gradually regulate what he did, until he finally could articulate and communicate what he was experiencing. I had apparently found a way to follow his directions so he could be physically contained, yet be in charge. I then tried to foster his new found capacity by asking him if anything came into his mind to show more clearly just what he was playing. He paused for a moment before telling me that he wanted to use my furniture to play a game. After constructing an enclosed space he crawled inside through a small opening and started to coo like a baby. He called it warm and comfortable, but began to feel that the space was so small he might suffocate. With some uneasiness he struggled to find the words that could accurately describe what was a somewhat vague fantasy of being smothered.

Perhaps it might have been possible to provide him with the containment without the physical restraint, but these words were not available to me. I did what seemed best, which certainly had a positive influence and in that sense was validating. If I believe that I am the source of, or capable of knowing for certain, another individual's truth, I think we would both be in trouble. I am only as credible as my ability to read what that truth is.

The purpose of psychotherapy is to create conditions that enable a person to have a life. This means the establishment of a relationship in which it is possible to express and have heard what is required for that to unfold and be realized. If therapists consider themselves to be the possessors of these kinds of answers it readily fosters a pathological dependency in people who carry within them an infantile hunger to be taken care of. In such situations the psychotherapy readily slides into being their life. There are many ways in which a vulnerable person's state of being can be invaded, only one of which involves some overt physical or sexual act. The imbalance in a therapeutic interaction that is part and parcel of the proper conditions places total emphasis upon the significance of the patient's experience, which has a tendency to encourage a dependent attitude. It can silently encourage a view of the therapist as an authority having the wherewithal to bring help and relief of suffering. Balance is brought by the therapist's realization, reflected in how the interaction is conducted, that the true authority rests within the patient. Thus the therapist takes full responsibility for the management of the conditions, while the steps taken are guided by the patient's direction for what is growth promoting. The resulting emotional atmosphere is one of honoring and respecting a patient's communications regardless of the particular form they take. It is in that position that therapist is one word.

Chapter 2

Pain Is Your Ally

At first glance it can be difficult to see how pain could possibly be a benefit to anyone. The discomfort it causes would seem to be a reason to think of it as undesirable, until we realize that it calls unmistakeable attention to something being wrong. Although the pain associated with mental and emotional difficulties has a different quality than that associated with insults, injuries, or malfunctions of the body itself, the mind is a part of the body and as such is guided by the same or at least similar principles. In each, pain is a pathway with the potential for illuminating its source and in doing so to gain a clearer idea of its meaning. This is certainly one important way in which it can operate as an ally.

Because many active bodily processes go on silently, with their quietness being indicative of harmonious, healthy functioning, we may lose sight of the fact that this is not always the case. Some destructive processes are also silent at first before their activity gets out of control. At that point they can be noticed from the pain they produce, and in addition be fairly well localized so that where to look can come more into focus.

The phenomenon of referred pain can complicate matters, since the identified site may not be the actual source. However, welcoming pain as a signal can give enough direction to discover the actual location. There are also painful sensations associated with healing that can point to ways that facilitate the process. This may mean utilizing a specific bodily function that may momentarily add to the pain, yet in the long run play an important role in attaining a healthy outcome. Therefore it is vital to discriminate between levels and qualities of pain, for the nature of the painful experience can provide useful information.

When pain is conceived of in a narrow fashion, one consequence is that no effort is expended towards discriminating between the various degrees and qualities of pain. Because of the complexities it is only relief, rest, or lack of activity that is sought. Often this approach is supported, not necessarily because it is known to be best, but due to concern that more damage may result if the pain was not attended to in this way. The damage that can ensue if the significance of the pain is misunderstood makes it safer to advocate being immobilized, or to give medication to alleviate the suffering and thereby diminish stress and anxiety. Entering what is often a very confusing and misunderstood realm, which focuses attention upon different kinds of pain and tries to unearth their disparate meanings, can be difficult at best.

These same principles are at work with emotional pain, which is created by unbearably intense feelings of loss, rage, terror, or humiliation. Hearing and following the messages these experiences carry can be a tremendous boon towards illuminating and healing the underlying wounds. In that sense the pain is referred and the pathway leads to buried and hidden mental events relegated to the deeper reaches of the mind. This also applies to very early, preverbal experiences, which when unbearable are deflected into bodily processes. There they act as a constant reminder of their presence, often expressed through a variety of physical sensations and/or illnesses. The particular site of the trouble, as well as the specific features of the pain involved, can make vivid symbolic statements concerning the nature of the causative events. Were the pain quieted an opportunity would be lost to open doors to their meaning, thereby casting aside its useful attribute.

These are all aspects of what could be considered as "good pain" meaning it is crying out for attention, expressing in a bodily fashion that something is awry. A full picture would also include its locale, along with some guidelines for its constructive treatment. "Bad Pain" would then refer to experiences whose causation is already known, and where the pain has no more to teach so there is no point in having to endure it. In that case having the pain alleviated can, and usually does, foster the healing process. Unfortunately this kind of discernment is not always made.

There are numerous examples of the body speaking out symbolically through aches, pains, and malfunctions; almost everyone has recognized such an experience at one time or another. Common phrases such as, someone being "a pain in the neck", capture the idea. Of course this doesn't mean that every pain in the neck has that meaning. Almost any bodily function or body part can be a receptacle for giving voice to emotional injuries, usually those having a traumatic impact. Until the mind has sufficient capacity to absorb and integrate the trauma it will continue to be exhibited within the body. The relationship between body and mind is then brought into the arena of exploration, potentially revealing the ways in which they are inter-related.

To know just when it is that a given individual can make use of the easing of pain in order to move towards a healthy solution, and when pain must be an integral part of that same goal is not an easy distinction to make. However, it is important to search for guidelines from the patient in making the determination. If a mistake is made it can always be corrected. Unfortunately such struggles may be bypassed, as though the only answer rests with the removal of the symptom.

The following clinical vignettes are suggestive of how encouraging the emergence of painful experiences, rather than finding ways to soften them, can be most helpful. They bring up situations that make me wonder what the outcome would have been if they were dealt with differently. Would we have had the same, or even better, result were medication added to offer periods of relief? I do not know for it is hard to tell. I do believe, however, that were I to have assumed that I was the doctor and hence knew best, and limited what I did to medication, it would not have been either good or adequate.

The first occurred in the treatment of a middle-aged woman. She had originally called for help since she was becoming increasingly depressed and could see no way out of it. She couldn't figure out what was wrong or why it was happening now, but it did remind her of a two year period of time during her late adolescence when she had been almost totally non-functional. All she could recall in looking back was of feeling very scared and hopeless and of not having the energy or motivation to do anything. After meeting and marrying her husband she came out of it, thinking the problem was solved. This relationship had then been the primary focus in her life, leaving her feeling extremely fortunate at finding a man who was warm, sensitive, caring, and who openly adored her. She, in turn, loved him deeply and was grateful for it. It enabled her to discover trust in human relationships. This was her explanation of what had caused her earlier trouble, which made it puzzling as to why this long forgotten state of mind had returned after so many years.

She was quite introspective and psychologically minded, traits she considered to be her most valuable assets. Searching for the true meaning of her thoughts, fantasies, and feelings was a constant preoccupation, and she was quick to notice hidden meanings in other people's words and behavior. This was also a significant part of her work as a free lance writer. In fact it was her inability to be in touch with her creativity with words and ideas that first alerted her that something was wrong. This writing block had persisted and she began to cry while describing it as her doorway to life and vitality. The door now seemed closed, making her feel like she was faced with a slow and agonizing death.

She then went into detail outlining the nature of her writing and what it meant to her, wanting to be certain that I understood it for she felt it held a key to her difficulty. It was the one place where she was able to feel what she called "passion". In all other areas of her life, though she was comfortable and secure, she felt dry and lifeless, with great hesitation and embarrassment she then referred to her hunger for sexual excitement.

Thus her initial complaint of depression was vague, but her reference to sexual feelings accompanied by embarrassment suggested the presence of more potential content than was immediately available. In addition what had triggered the trouble was at this point obscure.

Given such a situation I can't help but think of how easy it would be to simply believe that providing an anti-depressant would be a logical answer. Then she could be seen periodically over a short period of time until the medication was properly adjusted. Whether this would or would not have been adequate is unknown, but it certainly would not be uncommon for this approach to be utilized. In fact a case could be made that my not introducing it, at least as a possibility, was negligent on my part. However, her emphasis upon the importance of being psychologically minded, in conjunction with her drive to gain a deeper understanding of herself, was serving as my guide. Thus it was that I adopted a listening posture.

In succeeding sessions she noted her embarrassment each time she entered the office, which made her curious. She thought it must have some sexual meaning to be coming to see me, yet she felt nothing of the sort. What was most predominant was a very deep feeling of sadness. This led to a host of memories all carrying the same theme of being left alone hungry for contact, before meeting either rejection, disapproval, or severe criticism. At first they concerned her older sister and father whom she lumped together, viewing them as highly critical of her. With greater difficulty she brought up incidents involving her husband, a topic she avoided thinking about. There was a specific lack in their relationship even though she found him to be the kindest, most considerate person she had ever known. She defined it as an absence of passion leaving her feeling distant and alone. Finally it centered around her relationship with her mother, recalling being very close to her yet constantly frustrated and waiting for her to be available. These kinds of feelings came alive when she found herself being annoyed while sitting in my waiting room, before getting worried that I wouldn't appear. She imagined me preoccupied and unaware of her presence. My comment that it sounded like she was convinced that I had no room for her nor any interest in what she might need struck a responsive chord. Although the memories it brought forth were filled with sadness and anguish she felt as though a door had been opened.

At this point her responsiveness to the conditions of the treatment, her opening up areas of experience that had been largely hidden before, and the emergence of painful feelings associated with specific situations, suggested that I was following an unspoken direction on her part. It gave me the impression that it would be essential to encourage her capacity to be receptive to whatever would arise no matter how painful.

She had been raised by a series of housekeepers with one in particular being very special, for she had been actively engaged with her. By contrast her mother was a strange combination of being overprotective and completely oblivious to anything outside of her own private world. There were numerous occasion where she sat outside of the door of the mother's bedroom, softly crying, as she waited in vain for her to get up. At the same time, to her surprise, her ability to write returned. This made her feel relieved and hopeful as this obstacle to her creativity dissolved. It was quite striking to observe the increased clarity in her thoughts and memories. The degree to which she was able to receive what had been too painful and welcome its emergence into her conscious experience gave her hope, resulting in a larger capacity to contain great intensities of feeling. The dissolution of her writer's block said to her (and to me) that it would be counter productive to have introduced anything to blunt or deaden her internal world of emotions.

A shift then took place, beginning with her reaction to knowing someone I had seen in treatment. She became filled with extreme hatred focused upon her sister and father. Her fury then was associated with the idea that I might like the person she knew, making her aware of an ever present longing for me to love and approve of her, while secretly considering her my favorite patient. If I was fond of this other person, I would of necessity be critical of her just as her father was. I simply mentioned how hurt she seemed to be at the prospect of losing my interest, when once again a flood of thoughts and feelings lit up in her mind. Frequently she had trailed after her sister hoping to be included, but she was pushed aside as a nonentity. Eventually she withdrew, seething with rage, watching how pleased her father was with everything the sister did. The two of them were so much alike; smug, tight, emotionless, and viciously critical. Rage was directed to her father; all he ever did was attack no matter what she did or how hard she tried. She paused looking somwhat confused.

It was becoming clearer just how vital my listening attitude was in facilitating the bringing forward of these painful feelings. Very little was required of me, only some indication that showed her I was listening and what I made of it. Most important was for me not to impose my agenda in any way, thus allowing hers to occupy center stage.

When she became confused it was because she had noticed liking the sound of my voice, yet whenever I started to speak she got very tense as though bracing herself for some kind of criticism. It was like there were two of me; one she held in her imagination and one outside of her. Her face turned red as she was describing a fantasy of my hand reaching out to touch her leg. Suddenly she began to hyperventilate, with her eyes held tightly closed she whispered that she was so terrified she could barely breathe. An image had flashed through her mind and slowly the terror subsided. She then spoke at length of what had happened. A fantasy had started to form when "out of the blue" she became sexually aroused until she was gripped by a terrifying sensation making it almost impossible to catch her breath. It didn't stop until an image passed through her mind, which she tried to hold onto but couldn't. All that remained was the sense of bouncing on someone's foot, probably her father, getting terribly aroused until she was overcome by a frightening wave of uncontrollable excitement. The image and the feeling came together for an instant, before both slipped away. It was an orgastic like experience, too intense and frightening to be pleasurable, making her wonder if this had in fact occurred to her when she was a child.

A combination of my implicit encouragement of her following a pathway toward more painful experiences, along with my comments intended to shed light on the unspoken, hidden meanings of what she expressed, was bringing very powerful feelings and reactions to the forefront of her mind. She could begin to see that her hatred of her sister and father barely concealed her underlying jealous rivalry. My reference to her hurt initially had the effect of unleashing her feelings of rage at the idea of being criticized and rejected. Right on its heels a very powerful fantasy emerged, associated with high levels of sexual excitation and intense anxiety. It was also observable to her that she could just barely succeed in keeping it in the range of her perception. The feelings were so strong that defensive opposition was immediately mobilized. Nevertheless it was now clear that what had begun as vague feelings of depression, through following the pathway of pain, led to infantile experiences that were both frightening and painful. In order for her to function without profound limitations it was necessary that these warded off traumas be integrated within the fabric of her personality.

In the following sessions all that occupied her mind were the tedious details of the events of the day. Along with it she felt distant, uninvolved, and very frustrated. It was as though the incident had been totally erased from her memory. Even when I reminded her she could only recall a vague sense of having been frightened. To her chagrin and disappointment the writing block reappeared and with it a deep feeling of sadness and despair. The degree to which her difficulty mobilized protective measures to keep it hidden was quite obvious to her, so that she had come to welcome the surfacing of pain. It was like a guiding light pointing out where to look. There was no mistaking how much it served her as an ally, for without it, or without valuing the opportunity to hold it close, she was left clueless as to what to do. Were she to have continued to seek ways to further her numbness, or to distract herself when it threatened to emerge, the trouble would only have been perpetuated. Consequently there was a shift in her entire attitude, for now she was looking for ways to allow the pain to fill her.

She began to turn to me with questions as to whether I saw anything that could explain what was happening to her. Before I could answer a flood of thoughts would arise to occupy her attention. She finally noticed that she was almost devoted to insuring that there would be no room for me to answer. Her ruminating shifted to why she was closing me out and realized the intense conflict raging inside. She wanted to hear my voice hoping it would bring out her innermost feelings, but she recoiled in fright at the prospect. I reminded her of the two different ways she viewed me, and though she might be looking for my insightful words she might also be looking for something more frightening to reveal. She knew exactly what I meant as she found herself with a dim awareness of some erotic sensations in the background. Also she was becoming curious about me, with sexual innuendos unmistakeable to her. As soon as she moved in this direction they stopped abruptly, as though they were too dangerous to follow.

This was a good example of the way I was trying to follow her unspoken directions. By calling attention to the forces inside working against allowing painful experiences to emerge, I was aligned with her implicit appeal for help in facing anything without reservation. Much to her surprise she felt as if a heavy weight had been removed in response to my words.

Immediately afterwards there was a striking change in her outlook. She felt bright and cheerful, as well as sexually aroused. Along with it was a compelling urge to find a partner with whom she could be wild, uninhibited, and express whatever moved her. Several men she knew suddenly looked desirable to her, as she became preoccupied with having a brief passionate affair with them. Just the idea made her feel vibrant and alive. At the same time her writing block dissolved again, as a flood of ideas came pouring out around the concept of an irresistable, life-giving attraction of violent, passionate sexual contact. She was taken aback at this turn of events, for it felt like the full force of her sexual feelings had been released and nothing could get in the way of their seeking satisfaction. She wondered what happened, yet knew it had some connection to cutting off her curiosity about me. I reminded her of how frightened she had been of her fantasies about me, especially if they were associated with her sexual feelings. Apparently she found some relief in the thought of acting upon them with someone else.

Listening intently she fell silent before stating that she just couldn't see herself having such feelings about me. It would be too unbearable and frightening. Instead she was drawn to imagining herself with other men, and as she did the strength of her passion was wonderful. The similarity in the men she found attractive, however, caught her attention. They were all very bright, intellectual, arrogant, independent, and overtly hostile toward women. She couldn't help but notice that this was precisely how she described her father. This element only made the attraction more confusing. It led her to wonder what she had been drawn to in her husband, since he meant everything to her. Also she was puzzled as to why she felt no guilt whatsoever about her sexual interest in other men, or how she could so easily consider acting upon it. She placed special emphasis upon how kind and gentle he was, starting to cry at the lack of passion she felt with him. It had never dawned upon her before but he was like the caring, involved mother she had longed for as a child.

Early in their marriage she had considered having an affair, but shut off that yearning with the knowledge that it would be too upsetting to him. At the time it was strange because she reacted, without thinking about it, as if he would be pleased. It was as though he had been her mother and it was thus natural to seek a sexual partner. Shortly thereafter, while slightly drunk, she had been aggressively sexual with him filled with a surge of passion. He reacted by pushing her away and at that moment she just closed down, becoming resigned to a passionless existence. There was a kind of relief because it also made her feel safe. The only outlet she found was in her writing.

Over the years she thought of herself as content, even though underneath there was a lingering sense of loss. In speaking of the loss she realized what had triggered her depression. When it happened she was scared badly, but promptly pushed it aside and paid no further attention to it. Now in bold relief it came forward. Some months ago her husband had fallen ill, she had a transient fantasy that he might die, caught herself in the midst of it, chastized herself for being morbid, and then forgot about it. The next day she was unable to write and felt hope disappearing from her life. Her depression then became more encompassing with each passing day.

She was now bringing out how the underlying impact of an infantile overstimulating sexual experience (probably with her father), on the background of a troubled maternal relationship, made it necessary for her to institute stringent prohibitions to reenforce the repression of any erotic strivings. The consequence was in obstructing the flow of any instinctual experience and with it her passion and creativity. Her questions to me and inability to let me answer made her aware of the conflict. Thus she could see how much she wanted me to help her face and integrate what had been hidden for so long. The compelling urge to act upon the sexual excitement that was unleashed was troubling to her; along with it she felt vibrant and alive and her writing block was alleviated. When she was able to put into words just how much her sexual arousal was connected to the internal image of her father the pressure she felt was eased. The intensity of these powerful, infantile feelings had motivated her to select a mate who could strengthen her repressive defenses, leaving her writing as the only avenue she had to sublimate these instinctual drives. She then became resigned to this way of life until the idea of losing this means of support surfaced.

Gradually she found herself absorbed in fantasies about me, but this time instead of stopping they continued. She felt uneasy at first, anticipating a return of her inability to breathe. To her relief she could picture me in a sexual embrace without anxiety or even any noticeable excitement. However, she soon was bored because the possibility of it moving beyond a fantasy made it lifeless, uninteresting, and frustrating. She began to complain of it being a waste of time, yet she couldn't drop it. Soon her curiosity about my relationship with others entered the picture. She wondered what my life was like, feeling very uncomfortable about going into "forbidden territory". Once again she imagined me holding her, recalling her panic had begun with the idea of my touching her leg. With these words she could feel the onset of some arousal, which now made her question if this represented some way of reliving an actual experience with her father. Until now whenever she thought of him it was her later childhood and adolescence that came to mind. She had a vague recollection that things were quite different when she was younger.

An incident then emerged that explained a great deal to her. She had been playing with him by crawling on his lap while he laughed with pleasure. The game continued, she became overly excited, and wouldn't stop when he told her to. This instigated an enraged eruption in him. She now thought there must have been an undercurrent of sexuality in her excitement that he couldn't tolerate. Obviously it had a tremendous impact upon her. Later it must have been accentuated, for looking back she could see how threatened he was by her budding sexuality. This made her sexual feelings very frightening to her, something she had been carrying all of these years.

From this point on when her questions about my personal life came to the forefront she was able to give her imagination free rein, since she herself was curious. It evolved into vivid fantasies concerning my involvement with others, leaving her in a state of anguished longing having the knowledge that she was excluded. The idea was immensely arousing to her, but free of the panic that had previously cut it short. The fantasy could thus unfold and she recognized what had been so unbearable before.

Here it was clear that by following what at first was vague, having little content, utilizing the associated psychic pain as a guiding light, it was possible for all of these hidden and unbearable feelings to come alive within the safe conditions of the treatment. They could then be exposed to her more advanced integrative functions. Previously the anxiety was inordinately high, mobilizing defensive responses that kept them in the background. Now she had access, opening up a pathway for them to be included in her life. This was reflected in a striking change in her attitude towards the unknown, from one of dread to curiosity.

It brings out how important it is to not immediately introduce an approach that is devoted to the alleviation of pain, before there is at least some attempt to explore whether pain is necessary. At times if anything it may need to be intensified if geuine help is to be offered. A 20 year old college student who first came to see me in a state of extreme urgency is illustrative.

He tried very hard to describe what was bothering him, but simply could not find the words. All he could say was that he felt down and depressed. It was a familiar feeling to him because it had happened several times earlier in his life; though never quite as bad. Previously it had come and gone rather quickly. He couldn't identify any of the circumstances, or what was taking place in his life at the time, he was only certain of when they occurred. The first was upon entering the second grade; the second on starting the 9th grade, and the third when he began colleg. Now he was in his 3rd year, but it was more persistent and frightened him more than ever. He kept struggling to let me know exactly what he felt, yet all he could come up with was that he felt trapped and confused. Tears came to his eyes as he stated that it was intolerable to continue on in this frame of mind. In this way he seemed to be hinting at some suicidal thoughts.

I told him that it looked to me like he was communicating partly with words and partly without them, and it would probably take me some time to understand his language. He looked visibly relieved as I spoke, so I added that I thought he was trying to tell me he was worried about killing himself but feared saying it out loud. After looking somewhat startled, he said indeed such thoughts were often on his mind. In fact this was behind the urgency in his coming to see me. Now that it was out in the open he felt better. These kinds of things in his family were always left unspoken, yet he could see that it only made things worse. Unspoken it was always more ominous and threatening.

The rest of that session was spent with him giving me a vague picture of his family, introducing the subject by saying this was one area of his confusion. He missed his home alot, but was eager to be away. In this regard he placed great emphasis upon the concern his parents had for his welfare and how much they cared for him. He mentioned that he felt closer to his mother, whereas his father was very distant. While he was talking he noticed how careful he was in selecting his words properly. He wanted to make sure he was painting a positive picture of his parents, adding that he didn't know why that should be so important. Two younger brothers were mentioned briefly; one 2 years younger was extremely competitive with him. The competition was really one-sided since he avoided it as much as he could. He expressed fondness for a brother 10 years his junior. Smiling for the first time he remarked how good it felt to be looked up to by him.

This obviously bright and articulate young man was completely at a loss for words when it came to describing what he was suffering from. The fact, however, that he was openly relieved as soon as I indicated that everything he communicated was important and that he found it helpful when I put into words his unspoken suicidal ideas suggested to me that he was silently showing me how much he welcomed the encouragement to express whatever was present. This would certainly include his most painful feelings, since they would be at the heart of his trouble. Although it was conceivable that it might not be the case, or that it might change, it was at least an indication of there being no need to soften it at this moment. His entire sense of self immediately became more vigorous each time I gave any evidence of hearing, understanding and reflecting back what I thought he was saying. It hinted at his readiness to face what had been unbearable. I did have some clues as to part of his trouble. His almost frantic efforts to maintain a positive image of his parents suggested an absence of positive identifications, along with a tendency to compensate for it with idealizations. Identifications are based upon actual experiences, and hence on more solid ground in the presence of negative feelings; whereas idealizations are self created and therefore easily subject to deflation by the effects of actual experiences.

In subsequent sessions he noted how uneasy he felt when he talked about his parents. It wasn't so much that what he said was untrue, it was more a feeling of walking on ground that can give way, as if there was alot more to say although he had no idea of what that might be. It surprised him since he had always considered himself to be quite aware, perceptive, and eager to face whatever feelings he might have. He was now realizing just how much he had been running from himself. Nevertheless it was both confusing and strange to be convinced that he really had his life together, while at the same time being worried that he could easily fall apart. Although this sensation was undeniable, he still couldn't make sense out of it. I told him that I would reflect back to him what this sounded like to me and from his reactions and responses we could work together in discovering their meaning. I then began by referring to how protective he was of his parents' image, which said to me that it was essential for him to conduct his life so as to gain their approval. In turn this would make it impossible for any feeling to enter the field of his awareness that could disrupt the delicate balance he was trying to sustain. Yet the feelings would be there to continue making an impact, though the source might stay obscure. He listened closely before stating that he liked receiving this kind of feed back. It reminded him of being drawn into reading as a child; an activity that still persisted. Many hours were spent locked in his room absorbed in adventures and romantic stories. He hadn't thought about it before, but it was like entering a lively exciting world. Right now it made him think that the world outside of his door may have been too painful to bear, though once again he didn't really know what he meant. Only vaguely could he recall a measure of irritability in response to his mother nagging him. His father, on the other hand, was distant and unavailable, which he for some unknown reason preferred.

His immediate response to my efforts to show him how I was receiving his input was quite striking, strongly suggesting that I was on the right track in my approach to him. Furthermore in a non-verbal way he may have been crying out to me (and communicating) how much he required this mode if he was going to be able to face the feelings he found unbearable.

Suddenly his face brightened, for he thought of an incident that captured a feeling he had about his father that he had never known how to put into words. It happened at a restaurant between his father and brother. His father was criticizing his brother for poor table manners and when his brother protested it enraged his father. My patient felt humiliated at being identified as being a part of the scene. Finding the words made him feel like something important was opening up. When I then wondered if the things he was attracted to in reading might have anything to say about what was troubling him, he once again brightened up.

Here was more evidence that pointed out his need for encouragement in facing his pain, as well as demonstrating how the pain was an ally to him. It showed him where to look, and how to take in what he was able to see. What were at first only vague feelings began to take more shape, until he could find words for them.

The stories all had a similar theme; a heroic figure is at first beaten down and defeated by virtue of losing a special place in the eyes of a beloved woman. However, he emerges triumphant by accomplishing a courageous feat, which depended upon his being persistent in facing huge obstacles. In thinking about the stories he felt excited, but it also heightened the feeling of gloom and depression that was his constant companion. Pausing he lapsed into what looked like a very troubled silence.

His sense of self had begun to stand on firmer ground, supported by his feeling understood, which was manifested by his increasing ability to communicate what was happening inside. He was able to notice how hard he worked to gain support by seeking approval, opening up a feeling of resentment towards his mother and of being unable to identify with his father. The themes of the stories also appeared to be a symbolic reflection of what was starting to emerge concerning the forces shaping his development. They suggested to me that at some juncture in his early years he had lost a special place in his mother's eyes and was ever since driven to recapture that place before he could feel complete. It also sounded to me like he had been deeply injured by his mother beyond losing his place with her.

I waited awhile before telling him of my tentative reconstruction of his early years. I speculated aloud that he might very well have been the light of his mother's life only to have lost that special place plunging his entire world into darkness. It sounded like ever since he had been searching for some way to make his mother smile. He looked up to tell me that my words echoed loudly inside of him. First he thought of all the girls he had gone out with and how much attention he gave to making them smile. Whenever he succeeded he was on top of the world. In fact it was as if he spent all of his energy trying to figure out what would make them smile. One consequence was in all of his relationships becoming very difficult with very little spontaneity. While listening to my words he also remembered a dream from when he was 15 years old. In the dream he was a soldier who had lost a battle and was running from his enemies. Dashing into an abandoned building he found a locked room and knew his brother was in there. The building was deserted and there was an ominous sense of danger. He knew the only way out was to open that door. He had the strange thought that my words contained the key to the room, but had no idea what that referred to.

Ever since he was 15 there had been a repetitive pattern of forming intense attachments to girls, during which he only felt complete if he could have fun and laugh. However, if the relationship became more serious he would begin to cling and become possessive and demanding. This always led to the relationship ending, leaving him feeling deserted and with a pain so great he didn't want to live. It felt like it would never end. He tried to distract himself or to find some school project to occupy his mind to drive the feeling away. Most of the time this worked pretty well, for the loss would fade into the background. His most recent episode of depression was triggered by exactly this kind of experience. He had fallen in love with a young woman, felt on top of the world like his life was complete, and then began worrying he might lose her. His reaction was to cling tenaciously to her every moment they were together, wanting to spend more and more time. Finally it offended and drove her away. He was then bereft and devastated.

His response to my reconstruction appeared to validate my impression that the shattering impact of having lost an empathic connection to his mother with the birth of his brother, or the circumstances around it, was behind the way he had structured his whole internal world. It had left him compelled to repeat the trauma in his efforts to master it. The dream he recalled captured this same theme of having to open a door where his brother was kept before he could be free. The nature of his attraction to women and the regressive longings that were then unleashed brought out how actively he was searching for an all-giving nurturer. His hunger for an attachment that could stand with him, helping him to face the pain, was unmistakeable.

In this context he started to turn to me for answers to a host of questions. Almost everything he thought of brought a question to his mind concerning its meaning. It soon became obvious to him that he was searching for more of the feeling of contact and sharing he had experienced when my words touched him earlier. The strength of this longing made him wonder why he was so reluctant to find such moments with his father. He thought it was a conbination of his father being distant and of his being too embarrassed to either reach out or show any signs of neediness.

At this point he returned home for a visit and had a long talk with his mother. She told him about the events that had taken place when he was 18 months old. She became sick and had to be hospitalized for several weeks. Afterwards she had to remain in bed at home. At that time he refused to talk to her and showed a tendency to withdraw, supposedly expressing a wish to play alone. He had a strange feeling in talking to her, since they both were so matter of fact, that it was like they were discussing someone else. Immediately following the talk, however, and when he was alone he broke down in uncontrollable sobs. It felt like an abscess had broken open inside. He was able to clearly see how much these events matched what he had been talking about with me and what he had been living with each new girlfriend. Simultaneously he found himself not feeling so pressured to be the best in all of his school assignments. Slowly he was discovering what was meaningful and important to him, and what was designed to gain the approval of others. Along with this development he felt on more stable ground, for he could actually delight in the flood of memories, feelings, and fantasies that had become available to him.

His tendency to be internally directed and introspective was fostered and strengthened by his identification with my attitude towards him. His emotions were still labile, moving rapidly from feeling joyful and excited to despondent, but he was pleased at being open to the painful experiences he had always tried to avoid. He could see things with greater clarity and a deeper understanding of the circumstances that had shaped his life. The traumatic loss of his mother's involvement with him, in conjunction with his father's distance and inability to reach out to him when he withdrew, had a lasting effect. It was probably why my words touched him so strongly when he fell silent.

I then commented to him about the changes in how he looked at and approached the circumstances in his current life. First he stated it was a relief to be rid of the pressure he had always felt to be number one and succeed. He noted that it was also a little frightening to not have this goal as a means of keeping his attention focused. To his surprise he found himself feeling much as he had in the fourth grade. He vividly recalled how until that time he had protested at what he considered to be inappropriate demands and requirements at school. His belief was that he should be allowed to follow his own interests, which centered upon artistic pursuits. His parents considered this to be frivolous and were quite adamant in directing him to what they believed were more realistic activities. They only showed contempt for, and disapproval of, what he liked best. Great emphasis was placed upon getting good grades, doing homework, and preparing for life by following directions properly. He had always considered the fight against his parents as a rebellious attitude, which was coming to life inside of him once again. The difference was that now he could see he was fighting to have his independence accepted and approved of by his parents. The 4th grade was a turning point in his life, because he could remember crying bitterly with a deep sense of despair when he gave up the battle. Subsequently he was more reclusive, retreating into his books, and began to feel motivated by an intense pressure to succeed. Looking back he had turned away from what was most important to him, while constructing an acceptable facade.

He continued to recall his childhood years with the light of his understanding and it was startling to him to realize how he had kept repeating the trauma of the loss of his mother. This turned his attention towards his sense of his father seeming so unreachable. He was especially puzzled as to why he would welcome it. Perhaps there was something painful involved in getting closer to him. In seeing that pain truly was an ally, he approached the idea of facing whatever was there with an eager, open attitude. This was a product of his growing confidence in his ability to understand, alongside of the excitement he felt with each new discovery. I was viewed as a source of encouragement and enlightenment, in his words, to help him face his monsters. These were identified as feelings he found hard to recognize or acknowledge. For example, he could recall his brother fighting viciously with his parents and how exquisitely sensitive he had been in knowing exactly how to egg on the battles so they would end up with everyone being hurt. His mother would retreat in tears, his father would be enraged and out of control, and his brother would run off to alienate himself from everyone. He had to admit it gave him a sense of pleasure, at the same time that he felt horrible about himself.

At one point he turned to me complaining that he was stuck and couldn't get to the bottom of this vindictiveness, while feeling very uneasy in appealing to me. I simply focused on his uneasiness mentioning that it might be a clue to the answer to his question. It reminded him of a girlfriend coming to him for help after being date raped. Listening to her made him very upset, not because of any jealousy or of feeling helpless in knowing what to say or do, but because it had touched a much deeper feeling. It was as though he had put himself in her position and could feel what it was like to be so terribly betrayed. The feeling came alive as he spoke and he knew he had experienced it before. Almost immediately he thought of another incident in which a girlfriend had criticized him for being too dependent on her. This made him feel very hurt and defensive and in angrily reacting he had pushed her farther away. In doing so he felt an unbearable pain, like he lost something crucial that could never be recovered. He stopped and noted how all of this fit exactly with what he feared with his mother and why he hid all of his feelings from her. She was always contemptuous of any indications of weakness on his part. Tears welled up in his eyes as he plaintively asked, "What do I do now"?

I remarked that this must be similar to how he had turned to his father when he felt so hurt and betrayed. His face lit up as he suddenly remembered there was more to the dream where he entered the abandoned building with his brother locked in a room. The part he had forgotten was that he had stood staring at the lock, knowing he could get free if he could only recall the combination. In the dream he also knew that his father had given him the numbers a long time ago and all he had to do was remember. To his amazement he then recalled moments as a young child when he was with his father in warm and comfortable ways. These memories all carried with them a sense of feeling safe and secure. It made him aware of how much more possible it was to experience the turbulent feelings concerning his mother, when he was with someone he felt close to and admired.

In turning to me for help in understanding his hostility and in appealing to me for direction he unearthed the lost attachment to his father; the key to the locked door in the dream and the reason he couldn't handle the feelings about his mother's betrayal. Most importantly, however, was the change in his entire attitude towards experiencing pain. This could not be achieved through following someone's direction, or through some use of will power. Instead it evolved from his coming to know the value from having the experience of bringing clarity to what had been in the shadows.

Chapter 3

The Significance of the Future

Psychological suffering can be visualized in a variety of ways and, depending upon a given therapist's orientation, usually is. These different, and sometimes disparate conceptions of a particular disturbance, all have at least one thing in common. Generally speaking it is the effects of unknown forces at work in the mind that plague a person and create mental suffering. The trouble is not truly alleviated until some way is found to identify the source, and bring it into the field of awareness so it is no longer hidden or disguised. In order to be able to know something, however, it must first be able to be represented in some fashion. This is a vital concept, for much suffering is based upon events that have their impact during the earliest preverbal years. When trauma occurs before internal language has developed,it leaves a mark in the form of primitive mental impressions. There may then be no words to adequately expose its presence, but the resulting pain and anguish continues to influence whatever later developments evolve. The potential is thereby present for these crucial infantile experiences to be known and integrated, provided that they are recognized and given sufficient room to be fully expressed.

It is through bringing the light of understanding into areas of darkness that the unknown instead of being ominous becomes an opportunity for discovery. If some measure of anxiety still remains, and is examined more closely, what emerges are more hidden meanings of the unknown that have not as yet been illuminated. It is for this reason that the future, which is basically unknowable, serves particularly well for symbolizing and hence representing the unknown. In most instances when a person feels compelled to either fantasy about the future or be convinced as to how it will unfold, the motive grows out of an underlying fear of these unknown forces.

There is really only one way in which the future can be known and that is when an individual is driven to recreate some aspect of the past. Often it is expressed by a tenaciously held conviction that it is possible to know what will happen in the future, and of course it is then verified.

The anxiety aroused by, or associated with, psychic contents that are unknown is one thing, but one's attitude toward the unknown is quite another. Frequently when these experiences that have been defended against are revealed, allowing them to be integrated, the accompanying anxiety fades away. Yet a background uneasiness surrounding the unknown, though now more subtle, remains untouched. At first glance it may seem to be self evident that anything unfamiliar or beyond comprehension would of necessity cause at least a modicum of anxiety. It is common to have it taken for granted that anything of this nature would be somewhat fearful. For that assumption to be accurate there would have to be some ongoing internal event having the same attribute. Furthermore the fact that the experience is universal suggests that there is an element common to everyone.

So it is that all human beings carry within a sector of mental functioning wherein the impact of all biophysiological processes exert their influence. It exists at the boundary where body and mind converge, which always contains an element that is in the realm of being unknown (that which cannot be represented by definition also cannot be known). These bodily processes incapable of mental representation are nevertheless linked to those that are. The degree of anxiety aroused by the concept of the unknown is directly proportional to the level of psychic organization a person has attained. The more difficulty there has been in forming a solid foundation to the personality the greater the anxiety associated with what is unknown. Those who have achieved advanced levels of cohesion in their personality experience the unknown as a challenge.

The approach to both the unknown and the future are intimately interwoven, so that the dangers linked to the unknown can be eased by elaborating reassuring fantasies of the future. Conversely the future may be perceived as containing ominous qualities, thereby placing the internal danger at a distance. Perhaps most importantly the future provides a vehicle for symbolizing an internal event that has no other way to be expressed. A person may then have words to describe their anticipation of some inevitable future painful or frightening occurrence, which more than anything else gives clues as to what is happening at that very moment. In that sense it is not the fear of what will happen that is relevant, but rather the need to face what has already been experienced. Some temporary relief may be gained by believing it is the future, but the real opportunity resides in exposing its immediate meaning.

The threat associated with anything related to the future is most noticeable in those whose early years were characterized by a dearth of good self experience. One consequence is in an inability to buffer the impact of bodily processes, which then continues to operate as a focus of trauma. If, in addition, traumatic experiences are occurring in the outside world, as is usually the case in such situations, there may be no alternative other than to split off this key element for forming a solid sense of self. Even though the external trauma may eventually end, the impact remains as a continuous presence seriously compromising the course of development. This unseen dimension creates an unyielding stimulus always in the background in readiness to activate what is now an internally induced trauma. It becomes a dominant force so that everything, to a greater or lesser degree, centers around the effort exerted to manage or gain relief from the resulting chaos.

The treatment of a 24 year old woman who had been hospitalized on many occasions during her adolescence is illustrative. She had been described as having episodes of bizarre behavior, hallucinations, what was called "speaking gibberish", and being out of contact. Over the years she had seen a number of therapists, constantly searching for the right one. Her childhood had been a horrible nightmare, but she stressed how little good it did to recall it. The memories were all cut off from the original situation and her feelings about it. It seemed to her like others were more interested in the details than she was. She was convinced she had to relive her infancy and childhood and be reparented if she was to get well. This was what she was looking for from me. She knew it would take time to discover if I could provide it.

After this initial proclamation she paused for a moment before asking if I thought it would be possible. I simply said I would listen until I had some idea of what she meant, and we would probably find that answer together. She smiled and went on to describe her earlier contact with treatment and how sensitive she is to her therapist's "weak spots". With each one she had probed to see if they would behave defensively. Her efforts were always interpreted as manipulative and controlling and characteristically she would submit to this idea while knowing it wasn't right. Finally it would reach a point where she felt compelled to confront them and she would be rejected.

On this occasion she had been referred to me after a period of hospitalization, following a violent rupture in a therapeutic relationship. She had seen this therapist for several years and thought of her as sensitive, firm, and open to learning without being defensive. During the course of her treatment, a trusting alliance had been established and she was encouraged to express her primitive rage if she was to reach the feelings of a helpless infant. She sensed her therapist was not really comfortable with what was being actively promoted and that the therapist would have trouble tolerating a regression. This made her fearful of losing the relationship, but she was assured that this would not happen. Finally in desperation she brought a toy gun to her session. It was irrelevant that it was a toy, for the intent was to show her therapist the feeling of helplessness that paralyzed her. She put the gun to her therapist's head and demanded to be held. At first the response was a sensitive interpretation addressing her underlying desire to be safe and secure and she felt understood. It was the first time she could recall allowing such infantile yearnings to be experienced in a relationship. She could sense something coming together inside, making her feel hopeful about being healed. On the following day, however, her therapist had a delayed reaction, became very uneasy, and directed her to bring a friend to her next appointment. In that session the therapist was also accompanied by someone and told the patient she could no longer see her because a boundary had been overstepped in an unforgiveable way. My patient was totally overcome and the only thing she could recall was being in a mental hospital. While there she overheard people talking about sending her to the state hospital, and she was able to pull herself together enough to ask to see somebody and she was sent to me.

After our first session she reported a dream in which she had gone to see her sister's therapist who was able to know her better in one hour than she had known her sister in years. She then decided to show the therapist a very deep sore on her knee, but upon leaving the office saw the sore wasn't healing. She returned to her apartment going from room to room to turn on the lights and when they didn't go on she felt frightened and woke up disoriented, on the edge of "losing contact".

In our initial session I was acutely aware of the extent and seriousness of her trouble, and uncomfortable as to what I could offer. I was also uneasy because I anticipated her potential for a profound and malignant regression and concerned as to whether it could be adequately contained outside of a hospital. The dream seemed to capture her position at the moment. Her latest attempt to find help was questionable, she had to once again expose her injury, and when left to her own devices she was completely lost and overwhelmed. The dream also seemed to express her perception of my concern and with it the devastating effects that a lack of openness could present to her. Yet the construction and reporting of the dream, as well as the image of a therapist capable of knowing her, suggested there might be some threads of healthy functioning and latent resources available to her. In regard to the latter I was worried that they would be so vulnerable that they could only surface where there was no potential for injury and hence little room for my inevitable mistakes. In the presence of a profound disorder, there were hints that the integration of what most likely were primitive, infantile traumatic experiences might be possible within a communicative relationship. Her implicit and explicit demands for active involvement from me at this point were seen by me as evidence of deep anxiety at the prospect of having her personal space ruptured and invaded. The sense was of anticipating that some as yet obscure developmental trauma would be recreated. She was much too defended to allow a regression, and I was much too uncertain to know if it could be handled constructively. Therefore what lie at the root of her disturbance was in no way accessible.

She then became involved in probing for the limits and boundaries of the relationship,. sometimes playfully, but at times with grim determination. She would teasingly wonder what I would do were she to attack me, or my belongings, and was amused by my remark that I wouldn't know until it happened. Her worry was that I wouldn't be able to tolerate her if she regressed or worse that I wouldn't know how to help her in such a state. Many indirect references were made indicating that what she needed was for me to simply remain steady, while being open to receiving very primitive feelings and behavior. She began to feel both hopeful and frightened, but very uncertain as to whether she could risk being injured again. Through all of this, however, she held a firm conviction that in spite of feeling understood by me, the regressive attachment she required could only be offered by a woman. Then with great intensity she asked if I would refer her to a woman, convincingly describing her reasons. They all centered around her belief that only a woman who had been a mother would truly know how to mother her. It looked to me like she was presenting me an opportunity to send her away feeling as though something good and constructive had been done, while tacitly asking if I wanted a way out or whether I was willing to take in regressive experiences that could make me uneasy. I commented on my understanding of her question and she made it clear that this was her last chance. There was no way that she could survive another failure; she knew she would kill herself. Here she outlined what she visualized an ideal woman therapist would be like. In doing so she was defining her conditions for what she needed in order to be healed. It included warmth and sensitivity in a person who was well-grounded and confident in being separate, and who had the ability to foster the autonomy of a helpless, clinging, and dependent infant. While she was talking about these requirements her infantile longings were aroused, which activated what she called a "Black Mana". She described it as a vicious internal attack driving her to urgently demand that I give her comfort and reassurance by physically holding her. It felt like it was the only way to make it stop and if I refused she would go crazy or even destroy herself.

Despite her protests to the contrary I did not think she had to be physically held, though she did of course need to feel held by my understanding and emotional attitude. I thought this was her way of probing for blind spots in me, just as she had with others, but underneath it all was pleading for me to stay steady without being threatened. This meant it would be vital to maintain an intact, reliable treatment framework (not based on rules or prohibitions). She had already given much evidence that psychological boundaries had been invaded by supposedly nurturing figures during her formative years. If I were to adhere to her demand it might very well completely undermine the trust that was developing.

What she called a "Black Mama" sounded to me like a defensive force raging within her, in all likelihood patterned after the impressions left by severe preverbal traumas. It seemed to me that this "Black Mana" was designed to ensure that her infantile world of experience would remain split off, for it was the only means she had to preserve it from destruction. Whenever there was any movement towards expressing its contents the attacks became unbearable. Thus to heal it would have to be experienced in a relationship, but the "Black Mama" stood guard to prevent that movement. I thought the sense she had that she would either go crazy or kill herself, if I didn't comply and physically hold her, grew out of her need to recreate an enveloping pathological dependency. It was the only way she could quiet the "Black Mama". Under those conditions her split off (and preserved) infantile strivings would recede. In my thinking what she needed from me,more than anything else, was a way to diminish this destructive force before it would be safe enough for these elements of her regressed and true self to emerge.

She continued to insist that I hold her, while I told her that I thought she was trying as hard as she could to get me to participate in the destruction of her autonomy. I added that I thought it was a good way for her to test my trustability and encouraged her to stay with the feelings that frightened her the most, rather than working to ease or avoid them. In this way I was trying to present my view of the autonomy supporting responses that characterized the "woman" she needed to find in a relationship.

At first she just became more adamant, insisting that she couldn't find what was necessary with me. There seemed to be no doubt in her mind that she had to be touched by a woman who was a mother. She repeatedly expressed her belief that a man couldn't possibly have this kind of knowledge. She worked very hard to try and convince me that the healing regressive experience she sought could only be found with a woman and though my efforts were admirable they were ineffective.

What made me persist in my stance was her describing moments of doubt, when she could feel something shifting but she had no words to describe it. I considered this to be a crucial period for she did evoke uncertainty in me and I wondered if I wasn't making a mistake by not following her direction. I did consider the possibility and implications of doing so, since she so loudly proclaimed a physical touch was an essential step before she could move towards becoming a whole and separate person. In spite of my doubts I continued as the influence of the 'Black Mama" did appear to be diminishing and when it did get active she was able to describe it more adequately. It was an internal presence, beyond words, carrying with it an ominous threat that made her panicky. This description, for me, fit the attributes of a preverbal trauma and it also matched the impact of bodily processes on an immature psyche when there has been little buffering from good self experience.

Although my words appeared to have almost no effect when she felt the pull toward a regression, and the intensity of her demands to be held was at its height, a strong therapeutic alliance did remain consistently present. Furthermore there did seem to be a sense of safety silently in the background. I was not at all convinced about the validity of her demand and the vague feeling that something important was happening encouraged me.

She then had a series of somewhat obscure dreams in which she was lying on a couch but could recall nothing else. They made her think about why she couldn't use the couch; it was too distant, I would be disconnected from her, and she would get lost in an uncontrolled regression ending up in a hospital. It was too frightening to have me out of her sight, for she thought she would lose all contact with the outside world. I told her that I had an entirely different view of the couch. I thought it would bring me much closer to her internal experiences, more in touch with the deeper parts of herself, and that her present position of face to face contact felt like I was held at a distance where I was often out of touch with what was happening inside of her.

The next session she described how she felt dizzy after she had left, as though she were spinning around and had no idea as to why. I remarked that I was reminded of our talk about the couch. It made me think she may have been spun around towards looking at it in a different way. She then recalled a dream from the night before. She was on the couch with a woman as her analyst, as she became smaller and smaller, while feeling surprised that she wasn't frightened. In fact it felt like she was in the right hands. The symbolic imagery pictured her in a regressed state under conditions of safety and containment. I heard it as a statement that my interventions were enabling the necessary movement. Her attempts to recreate a relationship based upon a pathological dependency appeared to me to have a two pronged motive. First to protect and preserve a split off realm of infantile experience, and second to test my ability to recognize and support a growth promoting attachment. I thought my way of participating was diminishing the distortions produced by the "Black Mama" and resonating with the conditions she needed.

This was subsequently borne out in later sessions when it became patently evident that she had found the right "woman" in me. Gradually she began to bring out the world that her "little self" lived in. While doing so she felt enveloped within its confines, alternatingly feeling safe, comforted, playful, joyously alive, but then in mortal danger. It was a natural setting with sunshine and flowers in the foreground and a mountainous dark area in the distance. This was where the king of the realm resided. The king never appeared but his ominous presence was always lurking. She recalled entering this world at key moments as a child. These were times dominated by invasive physical and sexual abuse at the hands of a psychotic mother and supposed comfort from an aging father who would then use her as a sexual object. When the abuse was discovered she was sent to live in a children's home, and later during her adolescence in and out of a hospital. The gibberish she spoke turned out to be the private language she used when immersed in this split off world. She now noticed that she had unknowingly been playing out these scenarios in her interactions with me, while silently praying for a different outcome. Knowing how to hold her was vital; to have done so through bodily contact would have only repeated the experience with her father, and for me to retreat becoming emotionally distant would have made her feel responsible for the trouble as she had with her mother. Holding for her meant maintaining a proper distance; not too close, which she experienced as invasive, and not too distant, which she experienced as abandoning. Her pressured demand to be physically held and specifically by a woman who was a mother encompassed her dilemma. She did need to have a new experience of being held, particularly in a way that could support and foster her autonomy. Severe preverbal trauma had resulted in her only being able to make attachments in a pathologically dependent fashion, preventing her from integrating the impact of the trauma. Latent resources were vulnerable to destruction by even the slightest nuance of a lack of empathy, because of their resonance with the rupture of the necessary holding properties of a maternal relationship. These infantile experiences were in constant readiness to be activated, though they could not be verbalized until she found the sensitive "maternal" holding she required.

The distorting defensive force was patterned after the impressions left by trauma creating chaos, confusion, and the destruction of understanding. The similarity between this disruptive, frightening, presence and the ominous, dangerous king in the split-off realm of her infantile world was unmistakeable. The infantile realm had no access to contact with the outside world and hence the danger was more emanating from the impact that biophysiological processes have upon an immature psyche when there has been a severe paucity of good self experience. The "Black Mama", by way of contrast, had the same attributes but was created by her being overwhelmed by the invasive attacks of a destructive mother. In this situation it was easier to see how the impact of a preverbal trauma could be kept active by an ongoing inability to manage the internal source of stimulation coming from biophysiological processes. It was also evident how the absence of good self experience made the impact so shattering. The inter-relationship of these two sources of trauma had put this patient in a position where it was never ending. What then stood out clearly was that the events she feared most had already taken place, though she needed to experience it as anticipated in the future for her life to be at all bearable. For her the future could only be seen as terribly frightening, and it was the very fact that it is unknowable that enabled her to perceive it this way. In being unknown it could be given all of the attributes of the terrors she had endured.

This unknowable quality of the future allows it to be used as a screen upon which troublesome, but hidden, painful and/or frightening experiences can be played out. The difficult feelings involved can have some access to expression by virtue of anticipating them, whereas they may be operative at that very moment.

In less extreme situations this connection may not be quite as noticeable, yet upon closer examination it may be discovered. In all likelihood this phenomena may be at work in most, if not all, situations wherein the future is believed to be known. An example was seen in an 18 year old girl who sought help on the eve of her graduation from high school when her parents announced their impending divorce.

In my first contact with her I silently listened to her anguished expressions of feeling torn apart and distraught. At first glance it was certainly understandable that she would feel that way, yet she focused the most intense elements upon her despair, hurt, and fear as to what the ensuing months held for her. She looked to a future that seemed bleak and empty, lacking the support she felt she needed as she moved towards greater degrees of independence in her life.

The depth and intensity of what she anticipated seemed to me to be telling another story having a similar theme. Therefore at the end of the session I commented upon the obvious distress this decision by her parents had caused her, but it sounded to me like it might very well carry the weight of other traumatic events in her life. Also I thought it had special significance, because of the timing; just as she was moving towards greater independence. She was quite pensive as she listened to my words and spent the next few sessions talking about an earlier time in her life when she was closely attached to her mother. This had been disrupted by the birth of a sibling but more importantly in a change in her mother's attitude toward her. It was as though she no longer was important to her mother, which hurt her deeply. Her reaction had been to become excessively independent. In addition she was overly involved in intellectual pursuits and school achievements, priding herself on her ability to manage her own life. Significantly she then worked hard to keep harmony in her family.

Following a session where she was surprised at the strength of her longing for her mother, and the pain of feeling rejected, she reported a dream; "You were with me, watching my father and mother argue. My father disappeared and my mother turned on me trying to take my makeup. I fought to hold onto it and she hit me. She began to scream at me, about how jealous she was of the things I had. She wanted them for herself". She awoke from the dream with the strange sensation that she had understood something about herself without being able to put it into words. It felt to her like her mother in the dream was a mirror image of herself.

Both the direction her thoughts had turned to, as well as the appearance of a powerful dream, were indications to me that my understanding had struck a responsive chord. The particular pain and anxiety she attributed to what the future held for her had now turned to things she had already experienced. My image in the dream suggested that whatever had occurred between us had a stabilizing influence, something she needed in order to allow her intense rivalous feelings to emerge. I thought this was reflected inthe mother's jealous behavior in the dream. In spite of the intensity of the struggle there was enough regulation for the dream to continue, and more importantly for the resulting clarity to strengthen her entire sense of self.

Probably everyone has had such incidents arise in their lives, for it can be a healthy respite to be able to think of the future (something a little bit distant and far off) as the source of the trouble. Even though it is giving expression to what is probably already present, establishing a frame of reference that puts it off may very well ease the suffering at least to some extent.

Chapter 4

It All Depends upon How You Look at It

In traveling through life whatever a person experiences is determined by their perceptions. As a child when I looked up to see an ominous, threatening figure in authority, I felt intimidated. However, in gaining perspective, that same figure was then seen as being fearful, while trying to cover it up with an aggressive attitude. I now had access to more advanced functions within myself, enlarging my ability to perceive, and hence could move more freely. So it is that a person can possess a fuller grasp of the significance of a situation through achieving clarity. The result is in making more complete and adequate judgements. Living in the moment allows what is fearful to be feared, and no longer what echoes with or is reminiscent of hidden anxieties. Earlier memories can then be informative rather than influencing or even determining how something new will be perceived. What the person meets is simply what it is, nothing more or less.

Perspective enables a person to thereby experience what could be called "normal human misery". It may sound a little strange, but it is truly wonderful to be able to go through life in that fashion. Hurt, disappointment, frustration, aggravation, joy, happiness, pleasure, is then a part of being fully engaged in life and whatever that brings and nothing else. The baggage of old injuries is an enormously heavy load to carry; so to be able to move without its weight is a delight. The problem is that perceptions cannot be controlled by an act of will, nor can such a stance be adopted as a technique. A change in perception can only evolve as a consequence of having the experience of looking at things from different angles. Doors may then open that allow a broader viewpoint, leading to a deeper appreciation of its significance. It reminds me of my first contact with learning how to play golf. Everyone said that in order to hit the ball properly you had to approach the task with confidence. I shook my head in disbelief, for I couldn't see how I could possibly have confidence when everytime I hit the ball there was no telling where it would end up. There was no doubt about how hard I was trying, but I certainly could not pretend being confident. Then it dawned upon me that the wrong word was being used. Confidence could only come after I had at least one experience of hitting the ball well. What was probably meant was to be optimistic; meaning that I needed to be free of any preconceived notions as to how I would or wouldn't hit the ball. Then I could address the ball with a feeling of genuine hope that by doing the best I could the kind of contact I was trying to achieve might result. Being unsuccessful would not be perceived as a defeat, but only meant I needed to keep my mind open to learning and practicing. Lo and behold a time came wherein I did occasionally do it right. Once that was repeated with some degree of regularity, confidence could enter the picture. So it is with seeing things in a different light. It begins with recognizing the importance of perception, moves on to noticing just how something is perceived, and then allowing new or different ideas to be explored.

The powerful impact that infantile experiences have upon perception, thereby strongly influencing the way current events are experienced, as well as the changes that take place when perspective is gained, was shown in the treatment of a 48 year old man. He sought help for what he referred to as "falling into a hole". He had been a high-powered executive for a large corporation in charge of research and development. A few years earlier he had abruptly quit in order to go back to school to further his quest for knowledge. After finishing an advanced degree he suddenly lost all of his energy and motivation sinking into long lasting moods of darkness and despair. The idea of seeking help seemed shameful to him but he finally agreed to call me when his wife kept insisting that he had to do something. He just could not understand what was happening to him, for he had always been highly energetic and eager to learn anything he could. Whenever he encountered something that he couldn't grasp, he devoted all of his energy to unearthing its meaning. In fact, this was what had made him so successful in his work. He was extremely adept at getting to the heart of a problem and when one arose he dealt with it as a challenge. However, he had no patience with political maneuvering that was looking for quick solutions, because he knew in the long run this would waste time and be more costly. This was why he had left though it had given him financial security.

He finished school, was finally in a position to take charge of his life, and the bottom dropped out. Now he spent his days either sleeping or brooding and he felt trapped as he could see no way out. In coming to see me he did not know what to expect and he became somewhat confused as he tried to frame a question concerning what would take place. Would I give him some kind of medicine?, would I talk to him?, and if so, what would I say?, was there something he should be doing?, what was the procedure?. All of this tumbled out, while he had a perplexed look on his face.

My comment that I was listening for what was contained in his words in a disguised way, since he had made it clear that he didn't know what was troubling him, made him sit up in surprise. In a challenging fashion, half teasing and half serious, he asked what I heard. I told him that so far he let me know he didn't want a solution that ignored the cause of his difficulty and I thought it would take time to understand the deepest parts of him that were at this point unknown.

He laughed as he heard me playing back his own words, but directed to him a way that he had never considered. The idea of an internal exploration was intriguing to him, though he had no clue as what this meant, or where to begin.

This very talented man was immobilized by powerful emotions that sapped his strength and energy, leaving him lost, confused and filled with despair. All of his curiosity had been deflected into the outside world where it was safer for him to explore. Every nook and cranny could be searched for an answer, though he always carried with him a feeling of dissatisfaction, because the source of what he truly had to look at to be whole and complete, had been overlooked. This had to do with what existed deep within him, but the anxiety in approaching this area was so great that he had to develop a system of defensive maneuvers to deflect his attention elsewhere. Whatever it was that was buried within him was either too frightening, painful, or both, for him to face. Therefore he could not bring his considerable intellectual abilities and integrative capacities to bear, so that all of his advanced functions were used almost exclusively in the service of defense. When these underlying feelings finally did break through he was completely overwhelmed.

It was striking to notice the drive behind his intense curiosity, as though somewhere he knew that the unknown had to be confronted and mastered. Yet in the very place where this exploration was most important he was the most at a loss. It strongly implied that his curiosity simply had to be diverted from some (as yet unknown) threat in his internal world.

He quickly realized that a place to start was to describe himself as best he could, and so he spent many sessions informing me of his background. In the process memories returned that were so painful he was racked with sobs. When this occurred he would grit his teeth, exerting all of his effort to try and stem the tide of emotions washing over him, while cursing in frustration at his inability to do so. He had grown up on a farm in a very small rural community, the oldest of three children. At first he described his mother as a very efficient, pragmatic, rule-bound woman whom he admired as being a tower of strength. Although she didn't show it outwardly he always knew she was silently proud of his many accomplishments. From a very early age he took over heavy responsibility in managing the farm, accepting it as a matter of course. The work was there, it had to be done, and that's all there was to it. In school he was exceptional, far beyond his classmates, for he was extremely eager to learn. Often he raised questions his teachers hadn't considered, in which case he would probe for the answers until they were found. He had a keen, analytical, scientific mind and he approached every problem with confidence that he would eventually figure it out. Occasionally he created trouble in this area, particularly if someone in authority was defensive about being questioned. At such moments he would persist until he was punished for being insubordinate. On those occasions he would shake his head in amazement, as he could never understand why anyone would be worried about his attitude. In no way was he a troublemaker. In his mind he only wanted to learn.

This push for discovery in large part grew out of a lingering feeling of dissatisfaction that no matter what he found out it was not what he was really looking for. Up to this point his attitude toward me was not very revealing. He carefully measured his words and was obviously trying to be cooperative. After talking non-stop for a long span of time, he stopped to wonder if I thought there was any relevance to what he was saying, because it wasn't anything he hadn't known. He went on to ask if I got anything out of it. I began by saying it sounded to me like he was checking to see if I'd be one of those people who reacted defensively to being questioned. He looked startled, before recognizing that he had been wondering whether I would. I went on to say that I was struck by how lonely he must have felt when he was growing up even with all of his achievements, and I had noticed that he made no mention of his father. Almost immediately it was apparent that something powerful was touched, for he sat back silently with a pained expression on his face before he started to talk. He began by describing what it was like working side by side with his father. Very little was said between them, but there was an unspoken bond of sharing a common purpose. Primarily it centered around working the farm, though what he cherished most were the times they went hunting or fishing together. His father was a very quiet, shy, socially isolated man who practically never left the farm. A note of sadness entered his voice as he branched off to detail his life away from the farm, something he entered into with great enthusiasm and had a lot of success. He was truly a big fish in a little pond and used his physical attributes to engage in athletics, where his competitive spirit and desire to understand the intricacies of every sport brought him many rewards. It was a foreign world to his father, however, and never mentioned between them. All of this was a preamble to what had flashed into his mind in response to my words. He now tried to tell me about an incident he hadn't thought of in years.

With each word bringing forth deep sobs he struggled to stop the tears. At the time he was 10 years old and already handling many adult tasks. His father had tried to hang himself in the hay loft, and the entrance was difficult to reach and tricky to open. A group of men were having trouble opening it to get to his father and restrained his frantic attempts to show them how. He was left helplessly watching on the sidelines as they had pushed him away and wouldn't listen to his pleas. Finally they managed to bring his father out and though he was unconscious he did survive. Later nothing was ever said about it and he had pushed it out of his mind until now. When it occurred he didn't know what he felt, but at this moment the strength of his emotions was staggering. He could visualize the closed doors of the loft and what was behind it was overpowering. Struggling to find words he had a vague sense of imagining someone you can't really see fighting for breath, yet at the same time it was as though it was happening to him. In fact to his surprise the feeling was similar to what had been immobilizing in his current life.

This patient's character defense was designed to guard against the experience of any emotions, as all of his attention was directed outwardly. He focused his energy into finding logic and order in the world and was driven to discover the meaning of everything that was unknown. His talents and resources enabled him to be enormously successful in everything he undertook from the time he was very young; in school, athletics, managing the farm, and later in his work. When it came to understanding anything that had to do with his internal world he was at a loss. This was the area of experience he avoided, though it motivated him to seek out the meaning of the unknown. He had the right idea, but was looking in the wrong place. It was the unseen and hence unknown that was torturing him.

His concern about people giving easy answers and ignoring the need to search for the cause indirectly expressed what he anticipated from me. There was much in his background to produce

this expectation. He had painted a picture of a family environment devoted to practical matters paying no heed to significant
emotions, and had precipitously regressed in response to the
prospect of moving back into his old work patterns. Now, under
the containing influence of being understood, he did not have to
mobilize defenses to distract himself, and what was plaguing him
could take form and be expressed.

The traumatic memory of his father's suicide attempt served as
the internal image, which now surfaced and was available to be
given meaning. He could feel the impotent rage he experienced in
being prevented from coming to the aid of his father, as well as his
fear of losing this attachment. The potential for other more conflicted feelings to eventually emerge was present, as there was now
resonance and continuity within his personality despite the opposition from his defensive needs. Nevertheless the most disturbing
and disruptive factor was the sense he had of being suffocated,
which was behind the experience he had first described as falling
into a hole. He now found himself very curious about his reactions and behavior and in his characteristic style he kept a journal
lest he forget something important. In addition he drew pictures
of how he saw himself; one was of a superman who would show
no signs of concern over being rejected or alone. He referred to
this as his armor. Looking back over his life he realized how much
this attitude had been prevalent. An underlying sensitivity and
sense of humor emerged and with it a longing for closeness. It
made him aware of the distance he felt in his marriage, something
he created because he was so fearful of reaching out and being
rejected.

Periodically he felt stuck with nothing to say and at such
moments indicated an awareness that he must be hiding
something from himself and would turn to me for direction. When
I either remarked that he had already told me he didn't like

following someone else's agenda, or encouraged him to see what came up, he would go on to gradually expand upon his view of himself. On one occasion I referred to the way he referred to his mother in that he admired her strength and thought she always supported him, yet he carried a fear of being rejected if he showed any weakness and was constantly worried about being controlled. Before I could go any further he again burst into tears, this time allowing it to come forward. He remembered an incident that had been devastating to him. His mother had been hemmoraging from an open sore on her leg and his father in trying to help was making matters worse. At age ll he took over, put pressure on the sore with a towel and called the doctor. His tears came from seeing the vulnerability of his mother and the ineptness of his father. He had to manage everything himself. He just couldn't trust anyone else. The devastating part was the internal sensation of a heavy weight coming down toward him threatening to crush him.

It was now clear that his curiosity had shifted and with it he was able to explore his feelings and notice their deeper meanings. At the same time his rigid defensive stance was being relinquished and more of his internal world was coming into view. Consequently the source of his distress was more evident. The sadness in recalling the incident with his mother gave expression to the disappointment and emotional distance in his attachments and longing for closeness. Although painful this was not the primary cause of his suffering. The sense of being crushed by a powerful unseen force spoke to a deeper meaning and hinted that he was having trouble in managing his aggressive drives.

He gradually became more aware of how he had to keep an idealized image of his mother in order to protect him from a towering rage seething inside in response to the rigid controls she imposed. It was a terrible dilemma for him, since he also saw her fragility.

Therefore he had submerged all of his feelings lest everyone crumble. Everything depended upon his ability to be strong. This led him to what he considered the most difficult topic of all. It concerned his relationship with his wife, which he had avoided discussing. An internal state that had always been unbearable was involved. This was the first time he felt ready to bring it up. He then went into detail outlining an event that involved her having a brief sexual laisson and telling him about it later. The fact that it happened had hurt him deeply. His trust in the relationship was completely shattered, like it could never be repaired, while doubts about his manhood obsessed him. At times he also felt terribly frustrated and enraged; both wanting to retaliate while being afraid he'd lose the relationship. When these feelings quieted down he thought he would be more at peace if he could understand how and why it had happened. Subsequently he and his wife were able to discuss the matter and he did gain an understanding that explained it. He could see that she felt cut off from emotional contact with him by his distancing defenses and at the time they were living in a foreign country where she was isolated with no friends or family. His preoccupation with work had also left him unavailable. A male friend had shown compassion for her predicament, there was a frantic moment of sexual contact, and she ended it immediately feeling very guilty. To his surprise, instead of feeling relieved and reassured, he became completely obsessed. He simply could not shake loose from endlessly playing out a vivid fantasy in his mind, which was accompanied by unbearable pain. It consisted of an image of his wife that he was drawn toward, but as he moved in her direction he couldn't stand it and wrenched himself back. It was repeated over and over, causing him indescribable torment. The only way he could make it stop was to either masturbate or actively distract himself until he could drive it from his mind. He was afraid in talking about it now that it would start up all over again. He did notice the fantasy began to take shape as he spoke, but there was a difference. Now there was the knowledge of his wife being in a sexual situation with a somewhat obscure partner, while he stood on the sidelines bereft and sexually aroused. He realized that something important must have taken place for though he felt uneasy the obsession had dissolved.

Slowly and gradually the way in which he perceived these events, and hence what they meant to him was changing. As it changed and he developed more perspective there was now a means available to find a solution. The situation had been fed by all of the baggage of troubled feelings that had been buried during his developmental years. Now that they were being brought into view the way he perceived things was also changed. The incident involving his wife remained as a source of disappointment, hurt, and resentment, but now it was simply an unpleasant event; neither more nor less. The relief he felt was enormous.

The idea of everything depending upon how you look at it is particularly apt when it comes to considering the problem of addiction. Questions always arise as to how someone could be drawn to something that is so clearly destructive. What is frequently overlooked is that the addiction in all likelihood contains at least a small measure of something good. The compelling nature almost shouts out that there is more to it than some attempt to seek temporary relief from suffering or pain. Were this not the case the attraction would probably not be so powerful. It is precisely that aspect that must be identified in order to see the full picture. Only then can the addict perceive what is truly being sought, and with it the destructiveness stands out and may lose its power.

Addictions can be to a variety of substances, but also to destructive relationships. Often both are interrelated. The entire spectrum of addictions was exhibited by a 21 year old man who began his first appointment with an ultimatum. He had been in treatment, off and on, for 13 years and felt it had done nothing for him. A succession of therapists had given him support, reassurance, medication, and on one occasion firm behavioral directives. He stated emphatically he would try one more time with me for just one month and if nothing changed or he saw no hope he would simply kill himself. The depth of his despair was obvious in his demeanor until he began to talk about his violence, and preoccupation with being strong and tough. He seemed to come to life when he told me about his collection of knives and guns and how he didn't feel complete unless he had one with him. Often he was drawn to dangerous neighborhoods where he swaggered boldly as though ready for a fight. As compelling as all of this was it also frightened him, for he was always accompanied by friends inwardly hoping they would stop him. He didn't know why, but he just felt compelled to enter into these potentially dangerous experiences. He paused slightly before adding that he knew he also had a soft and vulnerable side, but it scared him to think about it. He was worried that if he ever allowed these feelings to come out they would completely dominate him and he would become like a helpless puppy. He also was concerned about the intense sado-masochistic relationships that were always a part of his life. He was sensitive to other peoples' vulnerabilities, drawn to viciously attacking them, while knowing full well it would end up with him being attacked in return. This led him to reveal his heavy involvement with drugs of all kinds, which he took in order to deaden his feelings and distract him from his fear of falling to pieces. In all of these addictions there was a small kernel of something positive in that he was taking some assertive action for himself rather than be left feeling helpless, needy, and dependent.

Overall the destructiveness of his addictions was apparent to him, but nevertheless they were uncontrollable.

In describing his family, first he mentioned how distant and estranged he felt from his mother, captured by an early memory of being alone in his crib. He had thrown his bottle out on the floor in a fit of anger, was crying out for his mother, but there was no response. It left him feeling alone, helpless, and trapped. During his early years his father was almost totally absent, though his influence was constantly there. Later he became a powerful force in his life, which had continued to the present. His father was always there to support him in a crisis, at the expense, however, of being belittled, disapproved of, and seen as inept and feminine. He worked for his father without a salary and money was given to him as needed. thereby encouraging a strong sense of dependency and obligation. He constantly shifted from one internal state to another and felt he could no longer stand to live this way.

During that month he put intense pressure on me to change anything I tried to establish. First in regard to the times, fee, and manner of payment. He said because his resources were limited his father would have to pay for the sessions and his father had agreed. When I reflected on how hopelessly tied he was to his father and wondered what it would mean to him if I accepted payment in this fashion, he protested vigorously that he couldn't pay for it himself. He sank back in despair stating that he knew it would be hopeless for there was no other way. After a pause he thought of an incident in which he tried to assert himself with an older man and was beaten down and humiliated. He had worked hard to appear competent and strong only to end up exposed as weak and ineffective. He also recalled many of his efforts to be independent, all of which had failed with him ending up crawling back to his father to ask for help. I thought these kinds of associations gave a picture of a pathological dependency with all the attributes of an addiction. It also seemed to me that if I accepted this form of payment I would be reenforcing this pathological state. Therefore I told him that it sounded to me like it would be vital for him to pay for his treatment himself. Several weeks were spent with his declaring his helplessness before he findally decided that he could earn some extra money to pay for his sessions. Almost immediately his concern shifted, for if he paid the fee it would have to be reduced. I indicated that I was open to that possibility, which brought forth a flood of indirect references to his fear of being seduced into a relationship where he would be a slave to someone's needs. I told him I thought it gave expression to what he thought my motive was for accepting a lesser fee. He was relieved, and a realistic fee acceptable to me was established. Now he began to put pressure upon me to prescribe medication. He couldn't sleep, was constantly anxious, and needed to get some relief. My response was to encourage him to talk about it, so I could get some idea of what it meant to him, which led to his describing in detail the many drugs he had taken. He laughingly added that he probably had been giving himself medication. I said that he might be asking if I would join him in supporting an activity that would work against his understanding himself, and perhaps insure that nothing would change. He looked touched as he was reminded of people in his life who had understood him and how much it meant to him. Often, however, they didn't seem to appreciate how desperate he was and their efforts fell short of really helping. When I indicated that I heard this as his feeling that I didn't recognize the depth of his trouble, or was distancing myself from it, he stated that he could see medication was no answer. However, he did feel confused and overwhelmed. Suddenly he began to demand more frequent sessions and along with it recalled the many times he was babied and taken care of whenever he felt like he was falling apart. The end result was to intensify his feeling of inadequacy and accentuate his need to cling leading to a vicious cycle of his making more and more demands. He hated this in himself. My response was to say that seeing him more often might very well mean to him that I saw him as weak and helpless or wanted him to remain that way. This triggered an angry attack upon me for being greedy and only wanting the money. He was certain that if he could afford a high fee I wouldn't question it at all. I acknowledged the truth that I would be affected by seeing him more often at a lower fee, though it still sounded like it would be feeding a way he had developed to protect himself that kept him from growing. Although he gave no direct response, he proceeded to get a better job, pay his fee, come regularly to his appointments, and arrive on time. All of this amazed him, for his history in treatment had consisted of frequent cancellations, lateness, and forgetting of appointments. Now he was even looking forward to his times.

It was far beyond the time of his ultimatum and the internal state that had dominated his life had started to be enacted in our relationship. He felt strongest and most effective when he was depreciating any efforts I made to understand him or when he elicited a reaction from me that could be taken as critical. These attempts to exercise dominance and control over me gradually became apparent to him, and when it did he quickly saw how it was an exact replica of how his father treated him. He also noticed how his inner compulsion to control my every move alternated with a deep sense of inadequacy, weakness, and helplessness. Heavy bouts of drinking and drug intake emerged along with a deep conviction of my contempt and disapproval of him. On occasion he came to his session under the influence of drugs or alcohol and searched for the slightest hint in my attitude that could suggest disapproval.

His addictive mode of interacting though dominating his life was beginning to show signs of being perceived by him in a different way. From being driven to seek this form of involvement and force others to participate with him, and from my attempts to shed light on its meaning, he saw clearly how much it undermined his ability to function. These moments of clarity allowed him to grow, while using resources he had no idea existed. He could then actually feel the value of being free of such an approach, and see how much more was possible when he viewed the world with perspective. The instability in maintaining his perspective showed how, indeed, everything depends upon how you look at it.

The following two sessions, several months later, give a picture of the readiness with which these shifts in perspective can occur. They also demonstrate how a more solid stance has to evolve gradually. In the first he was concerned with a relationship with a girl friend. He thought of her as a good person, and noted how driven he was to attack and depreciate her. He was always looking for a way to intimidate and control her. Whenever he did she retaliated, after which she felt so bad she sought comfort from alcohol and drugs. He commented that it was like watching a mirror image of himself. To me it also sounded like a reflection of how he experienced the treatment, especially in regard to any effort I made to try and direct his attention to it. He almost always heard my questions as being very critical of him. I then told him that I thought my words made him feel defeated and beaten down, so he would attack me and have a reason to turn to drugs and alcohol. As I spoke he looked pensive, before hesitantly revealing how frightened he was of being engulfed whenever he allowed himself to care for or love someone. He hated his attacking, controlling behavior, but he could see how he was trying to protect some soft, tender, loving parts of himself. The realization that there was an underlying meaning brought tears to his eyes, for he had never thought of it in this way. His hostile actions certainly protected him, but they also made him his own worst enemy. He wanted desperately to be able to love someone without having to deny his weakness or anger. Pausing again, while crying softly, he recalled a loving relationship with a grandfather who died when he was 6 years old. At the time of his death he felt devastated. Looking back it was the only relationship in which he felt accepted, safe, and like he could be himself.

The next session began as though nothing had happened in the previous one. He spoke of feeling inadequate, stressing how nothing was any good and nothing helped. His violence was continuing and would never change. He felt like he would never have a life of his own, he was just a helpless person who would always need to be taken care of and was incapable of managing his own life. Continuing in this vein he went on to describe his complete dependency on his father. His father always took care of him and he in turn felt totally obligated like he would never be free. While he was talking I suddenly became aware that the fee, around which so much had been expressed, had not been paid for the last two months. I had "forgotten" about it. I was thinking about the significance of my forgetfulness when he suddenly asked, "Aren't you going to say anything?". I knew he was alert to my facial expressions and must have noticed that something had struck me, so I mentioned that he must have seen that I did in fact think of something. Before I could go on he interrupted to express his fear of talking directly. He had seen a change in my face and was afraid to say anything. I said I thought he was calling my attention to his concern that I would be afraid to talk directly to him. I had recalled that he hadn't paid his bill and I had said nothing about it, and could see that might make him feel weak and helpless like I was encouraging his dependency. He had created such a powerful image of himself as vulnerable and easily hurt that as his bill was

mounting I had forgot. It was as if confronting him with the
unpaid bill would traumatize him. In forgetting I had been infantilizing him. He was silent before asking about the amount. I
answered by letting him know I thought he was checking to see if
i really understood, or whether I considered him to be incapable
of knowing the amount. What passed between us reminded him of
how he went to school expecting to fail and he always did except
on one occasion. This was a time when he decided to take some
courses on his own without letting anyone know. He was amazed
to see how well he did, but was too frightened to pursue it. It
made him feel like being completely on his own, which seemed
overwhelming so he stopped. He had forgotten about the bill,
though he did recall wondering why I hadn't said anything. While
expressing how good it felt to be in charge of paying me he proceeded to make out a check for the full amount. Again his grandfather came to mind, as he remembered being given tasks to do,
being taught how to do them, and allowed to do it on his own
without interference.

He had found it helpful when I pointed out to him how he
recreated his addictive relationships with me. It gave him some
perspective on the motives behind it and for the first time he could
see how these qualities were used to protect himself. In addition,
by virtue of experiencing me as a source of understanding, rather
than a means of supporting a pathological way of existing, he was
able to achieve a more separated and differentiated position. He
looked at the world through different eyes. I was seen as a person
possessing both good and bad qualities, which in turn gave him an
opportunity to recognize the good and bad qualities in himself.
His ability to see himself clearly became functional and the resulting change in perspective was experienced by him as a coming
together of what had been disparate parts of himself. In the following session he was immersed in his dependency upon his

father's dominance, and with it felt like nothing had changed. It made me aware of the bill and how I was supporting his addiction. Although he spoke of not talking directly, it probably grew out of his perception that it was I who was not talking to him about the bill and he was mirroring this in his reaction. He had created such an aura of helplessness that I would have felt cruel and sadistic to bring up the bill. Once this was identified and corrected the reasons for his retreat became more evident. For him to be effective and successful meant to be separated and individuated. touching upon an area of his greatest vulnerability. After i called attention to the part I played in reenforcing his defense he was able to act decisively. At the same time by moving into a more advanced and separate position his anxiety became more bearable. Being in charge of paying for his treatment brought with it the feeling of effectiveness and being free from his crippling dependency.

One key ingredient in a healthy approach to life is the ability to see things as they are. Since everything does depend upon how you look at it and will determine how a person will feel, it helps to define a therapist's task, which is to identify distortions and facilitate the ability to see with clarity.

Chapter 5

Who Am I? The Lesson of the Roller Coaster

A universal experience that I had always taken for granted first aroused my curiosity when a young child having his first encounter with a roller coaster asked me about the funny feeling " in the pit of my stomach". In trying to identify the exact locale in which I noticed that sensation it wasn't in my stomach at all; not even close. I placed my finger precisely on the spot and it was my belly button. This led me to ask others, whose initial reaction was to give me a strange look as if to say everyone knows it's in your stomach. However, like myself, they all then pointed to their belly button when they localized it. What a strange phenomenon; a part of your body having so little innervation would be the site of such an intense and unmistakeable sensation. It could best be described as "the bottom falling out", as though there was no place to be anchored. The sense is of falling into space with no place to land safely accompanied by varying degrees of anxiety; from mild enhancing excitement to so extreme it is phobically avoided. The universal nature of the sensation strongly suggested that whatever was producing it had been experienced by everyone. The combination of something everybody has undergone, together with its location at the umbilical cord, led me to speculate about the birth process itself. Without a doubt that was such an event.

The scarred remnants of the umbilical cord is precisely the place where an infant had been connected to its mother and then separated at birth. We can only guess how that separation may be experienced, but we do know it demands a whole new way of being in the world. The transition, no matter how orderly it may (or may not) proceed, has to have at least a moment of extreme disorientation. How easily such a primitive memory (or more acurately mental impression) could serve as a nidus, ready to be invoked with any stimulus capable of resonating with its essential character. I can imagine how the sensation created when a roller coaster drops precipitously would elicit the kind of feeling that now might be embedded in one's belly button as a body memory.

Another observation added validity for me in a somewhat indirect manner. I noticed that whenever I had gone on a roller coaster and that feeling arose I could make it dissolve by screaming just as loudly as i possible could. Every ounce of my being was directed into the scream with no holding back. In doing so the excitement of the ride became dominant, as the level of anxiety subsided to the point of disappearing entirely. Furthermore if I was reluctant to scream loudly, or held back in any way, the degree of anxiety was proportionate to how much I put into the scream. I also noted that I wasn't alone, for every roller coaster is characterized by the screaming sounds coming from almost everyone on the ride. It was as though everyone possessed the intuitive knowledge that their anxiety could be diminished by screaming.

In putting these pieces together it appeared to me that what was happening was a symbolic recreation of the terrible threats associated with the process of childbirth. A very primitive, immature, vulnerable, and undeveloped self, with lots of potential, is faced with having to shift the way its entire being was regulated within the womb. It could very well be experienced as being thrust into space with no anchoring point; a terrifying prospect. Anything in such a stressful state that could carry with it a sense of completeness or intactness could certainly serve as an antidote to the high level of anxiety. To my way of thinking nothing could better accomplish it in a short span of time than a loud scream echoing with every aspect of the screamer's self. It would be like a strong reminder that they were a whole person, whether it was fully realized or not. In the brief moment of the scream the threat is alleviated.

Another observation, at first seemingly unrelated, involved my noticing how affirming and reassuring it was for a person feeling threatened to be able to openly and forcefully speak their mind. Conversely, the particular threatening situation was exaggerated when they either couldn't speak their mind or didn't know what was in their mind to say. It seemed to me then that the two experiences, on the surface so disparate, were very much related. With this realization of the similarity between the roller coaster lesson, and the effect of being silenced, came a direction; the antidote to a threatened self was to find and articulate whatever needed to be spoken.

The treatment of a 45 year old divorced woman demonstrated how her attitude toward the unknown changed from one of panic to manageable anxiety, and with it the recognition of how vital it was to speak her mind. The deep appreciation of its value was a significant factor in enabling the change. It was the equivalent of a loud scream.

Initially she was in tears only able to state that her whole world had collapsed. She saw herself suspended in space facing nothing but sheer terror; falling forever cutoff from all support and human contact. Her entire life had been spent trying to distract herself from this feeling, largely succeeding until recently. Looking back she could see that the only answer she had found involved holding onto illusions, which had led her into a very abusive marriage. It had finally reached a point where she could no longer deny its destructiveness. After getting a divorce she tried to develop a career, but nothing worked any longer. Over the years she had seen a number of therapists, who had helped for short periods of time by encouraging her to direct her attention into a variety of activities. She followed these directions and did find some relief, readily accepting the idea that she was better and the problem was solved. At the same time she knew full well that the feeling enveloping her now was always lurking in the shadows. Whenever she was faced with any uncertainty, lack of purpose, or anything unknown this inner sense of abject terror surfaced. She then felt hopelessly trapped since she had no way of understanding the source or even of finding words to express it.

This patient appeared to be afftected by archaic internal experiences, probably pre-verbal in nature, which hadn't been able to take the form of thoughts or mental imagery. They were most likely unrepresentable and hence unthinkable, expressed primarily in her feeling overwhelmed, cut off from all contact with the world. The similarity to the sensation of plummeting downward in a roller coaster might not be noticeable at first glance, because the circumstances are so different and the resultant level of anxiety so high. In one there is an element of choice so the experience can be avoided, as well as an end being in sight. The other arises unbidden from within, placing her at the mercy of an experience having the attributes of a trauma. There is no sense whatever of excitement or fun, and no end in sight. Yet there exists in the two situations the theme in common of a threat to the sense of self.

Somewhat surprisingly she felt both relieved and hopeful when I told her I had no idea what all this meant. I added that I thought whatever she could say about her experience was helpful, including her panic and despair. I would listen, try to understand, and let her know what I made of it as we went along.

The early sessions were filled with her worries about her life, the effects of her divorce, her limited income, and lack of a career. She felt there was absolutely nowhere she belonged, adding to her sense of being lost, cut off, and almost continuously terrified. Interspersed with these anguished descriptions of her adult life, fragments of her early history came through. She was the only child of an extremely invasive, viciously attacking mother and an aloof, critical father. The only time interest was shown in her it was to gain the attention and admiration of others, whereas her needs and desires were viewed as evidence of her greedy nature. The picture she presented was of a total lack of parental support, as she was left to her own devices in dealing with everything. It certainly made it explicable that anything arising within her elicited high levels of anxiety. Remarks I made to this effect seemed quite useful, for she responded by beginning to remember her dreams and to recall painful childhood incidents leading to her isolating herself from the outside world. Much of her time was spent engrossed in books, since contact with other children and social situations were avoided. Looking back she realized how terrified she was of almost everything.

I noticed her anxiety was alleviated when I was receptive to her input, able to be silent while I tried to put together whatever she expressed, and then periodically give my impression of how I understood its meaning. It didn't seem to matter much when I was inaccurate, but when I was in tune more would come forward. It appeared most important that I participate with her. When words came to her the relief she felt was almost palpable, for she had never been able to articulate very well what was happening inside. Not surprisingly the slightest attempts on my part to probe, or even to ask questions in order to clarify something, were taken by her as invasive triggering either intense anger or anxiety. At those moments she would once again feel cut off and alone. At this point the most significant experiences for her centered around her increasing ability to speak her own mind, a somewhat distant spin-off of screaming loudly.

Dreams gradually became increasingly available and for some time became the focus of her treatment. They served as a central nidus, evoking associations that brought forth memories and ideas that had not been accessible before. In addition as she was recognizing the meanings of the symbolic imagery, she was struck by how much she knew without realizing it. She noticed that in a dream she was curious rather than frightened, quite in contrast to how frightened she was in a waking state. It reminded her of her search for an editor to help put together the chapters of a book she was writing, and immediately saw the connection to how she experienced my role in her treatment. Many childhood memories of having to hide her abilities also returned, since any sign of creativity, independence, or speaking her mind was attacked. She had spent a lifetime hiding from others, only able to be resourceful when giving an idea to someone else. She continued to feel frightened of being alone, but now instead of a terrifying sensation of falling into a void she noticed it centered upon feeling vulnerable to being attacked. She connected it to the times I was unempathic, which made her feel the same way. That night she had a dream that seemed like a turning point to her. A big hairy man was raping a woman in front of a large crowd. She picked up a knife stating emphatically that he had better stop. At first the dream made her think of her abusive marriage and fear of being assertive. Nevertheless she could feel a change in her attitude, in that she was able to make an unmistaeable statement of her refusal to be a victim. In shouting out those words without holding anything back there was an immediate alleviation of her panic. Though still somewhat fearful of the consequences, she began to feel confident about doing it again. She was truly finding her own voice.

The lesson of the roller coaster symbolizes the importance of shouting out loud, so who and what one is resonates throughout and hence has the potential of being known. However it is not always possible for to know, or even have access to or resonance with, the deeper reaches of one's mind. Under such conditions speaking out would be like a half-hearted scream, only making the anxiety worse. Therefore even though many words may be present, if the key elements cannot be spoken the threat persists. So it was with a 17 year old boy who was originally referred to me as a last resort. He had been to three other therapists of differing orientations who determined that his particular phobia was not treatable. His family doctor then suggested he see a psychoanalyst and he called me. He was bright, extremely intellectual, and immediately began to speak of the outrage he felt in not being able to overcome his fear of being in a classroom with other students. It had reached such an extent that he was completely unable to attend school and felt helpless in finding a way to deal with it. Finally he had to receive home teaching. Now he was concerned primarily due to an acute and pressing problem. He had been given a scholarship to college, which he would lose if he didn't take an upcoming test. The time kept getting closer and he felt desperate, for he still was unable to think of going back to school much less enter a classroom to take the test.

Without pausing he went on to talk about why he was so outraged. He had always considered himself to be smart and accustomed to "commandeering" the classroom. Therefore it came as an enormous surprise to him the very first time he was too frightened to enter. Earlier he had just revelled in going to school and now he felt like his whole life was ruined. It did remind him of when he was younger and going to school was painful. At the time he was teased about being a brain and felt like an outcast. Over the years this got much better as his peers became more mature and he wasn't teased as much. He thought it also had to do with his being an excellent athlete, since this diminished the extent to which he was teased. This led him into describing his athletic skills and accomplishments. A worried expression appeared on his face as he did so, which deepened as he went on, until he paused to voice his concern that I would misunderstand and see him as bragging and arrogant. He wanted to make sure it was clear to me how hard he was working to give an accurate picture of himself. In order to do that he had to describe his exceptional abilities.

Although this young man was very articulate and by implication was emphasizing how readily he spoke his mind, yet what frightened him so terribly was in no way accessible to him or visible to me. Thus he couldn't enter a setting where something was demanded of him, if nothing else showing him it symbolized something terrifying to him. Certainly it was not unlike someone who is terrified, or even phobic, of getting on a roller coaster. In that situation the person might assume they knew what was frightening, for the potential for danger was clearly in view. This patient, however, seemingly had nothing to pin it on and so it appeared mysterious. In order to speak his mind effectively the underlying significance of the school situation would have to emerge. Nevertheless there were some hints. The impending separation from home, for example, might have precipitated the panic, though as yet that was not evident. The outrage he felt underscored the high position he held himself in, and in this regard his worry that I would see him as arrogant was also speaking to something vital. My impression was that it was heralding his hypersensitivity to even minimal lapses in empathy, which suggested that traumatic ruptures in empathy may have been a factor in his developmental years. Along these lines the emphasis he put on his special skills implied a fear of being envied by others, as well as a fear of being attacked for displaying them. It was as though he anticipated and was preparing himself for being criticized and misunderstood.

His thoughts then turned to the other therapists he had seen. One tried to desensitize him from his phobia, but was unsuccessful. This led him to telling me the details. He approached the classroom, felt sick to his stomach, had a blinding headache, and had to return home. The first therapist encouraged him to visualize the experience and when he was completely unable to comply he was discharged. He next went to see a nutritionist who treated him with a variety of foods and vitamins and that seemed to help. It took place during the summer and when he felt stronger he thought the problem was solved. School began and his phobic reaction if anything was more pronounced. He then saw a third therapist who directed him to exercise his will power, making him feel totally misunderstood, so he left. By this time he was convinced he had a serious physical illness and so he went to see his internist. When he couldn't take a series of G.I. tests, the internist referred him to me.

At this point he stopped to ask if I could help, and more importantly if it could be within a few weeks. The college test was soon so there was very little time. His anxiety and attention were focused almost entirely on his body sensations, which made me think he was so humiliated he could hardly bear to reveal how frightened he was, perhaps even to himself. Everything he feared was centered upon the classroom, which he then phobically avoided. At the same time he was struggling to intellectualize the problem, trying mightily to master the feelings with his thinking. His associations to the other therapists gave an indication of how he reacted with flight when he was not understood, especially if pressure was put on him to confront the very situations that terrified him. Thus his question to me seemed like a tentative reaching out to see if he would meet with a similar fate. To approach him that way would be akin to trying to force someone who was terrified of a roller coaster on to the ride. Clearly it would lead nowhere. That same person, able to really grasp that to really scream with every ounce of energy would erase the anxiety, might be able to decide to take that step on his own. The equivalent in this situation would not be as simple, but the principle would be the same. Thus to offer him an opportunity to discover the source of his terror, and to provide him with the proper conditions to express it and feel the value, would be indicated.

I had been thinking of his imminent graduation when he would be faced with the reality of separating from his home, and considered what this might represent to him. Everything he had said thus far had indicated that an extensive period of therapeutic contact would be necessary if he were to be helped, which made me wonder if he didn't either know it or at least sense the possibility. I thought he might be probing to see if I really understood and could help him hear this internal message. Therefore I commented upon his desperation and wondered aloud whether he could be asking if I was in a hurry. After a short pause he began to talk about what the examination meant to him. He assumed I thought he was doing all of this for someone else, so that I must think he was being pressured and didn't want to take the exam nor go to college. He wanted to assure me with all of his heart and soul that more than anything he wanted both to take the test and to go to school. It was essential that I understand that about him. After pausing again, he asked if what I meant was that there could be something going on inside of him that he knew nothing about and I was listening for it and hearing it. I replied that it sounded like he was aware that he didn't hear himself very well and needed help with that. He quickly stated how much he agreed with that and regular sessions were scheduled.

I was offering him a chance to go on with no knowledge of how long it would take. Whatever occurred would be determined by how accurately I could read what he communicated and play it back to him so he could read his own messages.

During the early sessions he often turned to look at me whenever he spoke. This had never happened to him before. He always had something to say. It reminded him of lying in bed at night, feeling frightened like everything was out of control. It was strange to feel scared now, because nothing came into his mind. All he could notice was the pressure to talk, which was exactly like the time pressure he felt in his life. It was a relief to him to discover that he was fighting against things coming to mind. even though he didn't know what they were, since it made him feel more in charge of what was taking place. Shortly thereafter he recalled the thoughts he had while he was in bed. They didn't seem to be as troubled and chaotic as before, but it consisted of a very clear sensation that he was in danger. It felt like hearing footsteps and imagining that something in the dark was about to harm him.

He had become more introspective and discriminating in observing himself. This said to me that our interaction was supporting what he needed to grow, although the nature of what was disturbing was still not discernible. However, along with his developing a more insightful awareness of his defensive attitude, something lacking before, he was seeing the danger resided within. The following session took place just prior to his college exam. He came in very agitated, explaining that he had found a way to take the exam, but it required a note from me. Once he had the note he could be given the exam by himself and wouldn't have to go into the classroom. With some uneasiness he asked if I would write it, and I simply remarked lets see what comes to mind. He then thought of one example after another of having been put down and considered to be incapable. Whenever he finished something it was always belittled. Both of his parents constantly criticized him for being weak and infantile. Suddenly he stopped to ask, "You haven't answered me. What about the note?". I said it looked to me like he was asking whether I too considered him to be ineffective. He became silent before expressing a tremendous letdown and feeling of disappointment. Finally he had found a way to take the test and my words were implying that I wouldn't give him the note. It was like I thought in doing that I would hurt him. Once again he lapsed into silence. The session ended and as he was leaving he said, "I guess what you're really saying is I'll have to wait and see what I do about the exam. If I really trust myself it isn't important whether I take the exam or not. It's what I do that counts and I need to understand that".

At a point when I began to question myself as to whether I was adopting a proper posture and hearing his message correctly, and hence not immediately writing the note, his insightful comment encouraged me to maintain that stance. Under the pressure of seeking a quick answer he was actively feeling disappointment with my hesitation. Deeper down I thought he was directing an appeal to me to remain steady, so that I could help him hear.

That night I received a call from his parents. He had just stormed out of the house and they wanted advice as to what to do. I told them I wasn't able to discuss it. This session took place shortly afterward. He began by referring to his parents' call and my response. After leaving the session he had gone home to type an essay on what it meant to look at your life in a new way. It reminded him of a book he had read, especially one of the characters who had done something beautiful. He had followed his heart, which so offended everyone that the wrath of society descended upon him leading him to his death. While working hard to put into words what it meant to him to follow his heart he began to type, just as his mother asked him to do a chore. He ignored her, so she pulled out the sheet. To his surprise and chagrin he exploded, pushed her, felt devastated, and ran out of the house to be alone. He was profoundly shaken by the dawning realization that powerful emotions were buried deep within him. He knew now that they were behind his symptoms.

Once again it looked like he was validating my impression that I was hearing him, and he was discovering some of what had been in the depths of his mind. It then opened the door for him to speak his mind, something not possible before.

Now he began to talk about the character in the book that had touched him. He couldn't get it out of his mind. He was aware of his feelings in a way that he had never experienced before, and had never been able to put into words. When it was quiet he could hear the voice of his mother inside of him, like she was saying, "I'm going to surround you and swallow you up". It made him feel like he would either die or kill himself. He noted that he was nauseated, as though he was trying to get rid of these frightening inner sensations but couldn't. It felt like he was attached to them, as well as to his mother and father, in such a way that he could neither reject nor assimilate them. It was striking to him, and to me, to see how deeply in touch he had become with very powerful feelings. In this sense he was finding himself and in speaking he felt more complete. However, much like a reluctant scream, he knew there was more to be said.

His thoughts turned to the book, as he noticed how he avoided any mention of the details. He wanted to believe that I knew the story already so he wouldn't have to go into it, sensing that the specifics were connected to some vulnerable part of himself. It felt so vulnerable that talking about it would make him retreat instead of moving forward. At this moment it looked to me like he was standing at a crossroad. He saw the value of being open to whatever came forth and communicating it as best he could, but now also felt a tendency to back away. Although it went unspoken, my impression was that he was looking for me to add some input at this point to determine the direction he would take. I was silent, feeling this was the best way to implicitly encourage him to continue on the path he was following. He hesitated for a moment before stating that the character he identified with had a sexual relationship with the wife of a lordly figure, who then became pregnant and had a baby. He saw the husband much as he saw his father, and himself as having had a hidden, special relationship with his mother. Mentioning a younger brother for the first time, he described watching him with his mother. They had a special bond that gave him an eerie feeling, like he wanted the same thing for himself and was experiencing it vicariously. It also made him think that he might have been similarly involved when he was younger. Just thinking about it made him very uneasy.

In the beginning of his treatment he was able to notice that it was his own feelings that frightened him the most. Later he connected them to his symptom, but it wasn't until he exerted pressure upon me to write a note that the defenses he utilized to prevent him from opening up his deepest feelings became apparent. The phobia itself cried out to how threatened he felt, so my writing of the note would in essence serve to reenforce his defensive stance. Consciously he was looking for me to gratify his search for comfort, safety, and security, which in his view could allow him to reach a desired goal. Such a move would have been regressive and infantilizing. His associations pictured how my participating this way could undermine his autonomy, eroding his ability to grow, while deeper down being experienced as demeaning. My approach to work towards understanding his wish, instead of gratifying it, had the ultimate effect of diminishing his anxiety. Now he was revealing the features of an internal infantile conflict, which had been vigorously defended against. At first his allusions to the character were quite abstract, but he couldn't help but notice how he avoided the main theme. In elaborating upon the details he was expressing the emergence of an erotically tinged attachment to his mother, which made him feel very vulnerable. He now stood at the threshold of facing these frightening feelings and in doing so was at last speaking his mind.

Chapter 6

What is the Meaning of a True and/or False Self?

It is such a common occurrence in human interactions for words to be used, which both parties assume have the same meaning to each. Nothing could be further from the truth. This can be shown in a myriad of different circumstances, but nowhere is it more confusing (and at the same time more important) than in trying to describe the meaning of the word self. Certainly a clear and adequate definition has to be available before it is even possible to approach the topic of what constitutes a true or false self. These terms are often used as though their meaning is self evident, yet on closer examination any clear distinction begins to become less distinct. For example, what is meant by a true self? Does it refer to what a person is and nothing else? How is it possible then for anyone to be exhibiting a false self? Anything a person thinks or does is there to be a part of who and what they are, so how can it be false? Yet these are useful concepts in gaining an understanding of another person, for they do illuminate many aspects of human experience.

Everyone has been in the position of not fully expressing themselves in certain situations, often keeping what they truly feel deliberately hidden. In many social encounters, or in responding to questions, who has not said what was expected. Furthermore a good argument can be given for being selective in what one says when, how, and to whom without it being evidence of difficulty or trouble. In fact, depending upon the circumstances, speaking openly and truthfully could very well be bad judgement. Politeness is an integral aspect of most social interactions, and yet in being polite a person is undoubtedly not being true to themselves. One could say the situation doesn't call for such openness and hence our responses are in that way appropriate. This might be an instance illustrating where a false self might represent a healthy adaptation. Of course it also raises a question as to if one can be healthy and false. Clearly there is something not quite accurate in the terms true and false as applied to the self.

Perhaps it would be more to the point if a false self were called an incomplete self. When an individual is not being true to their genuine feelings, or may not have access to them, this description seems to me to be more accurate. Usually when speaking of the self, it includes a person's identity, the nature of their character, their unique thoughts and feelings, and the particular qualities that comprise their way of being in the world. All people in certain situations will hide some or all of these components, sometimes working to create a favorable impression, often without regard for whether it is true or not. This may be carried to such an extreme that the entire focus is upon determining what others expect or anticipate, and then molding themselves to fit that image.

When others wishes are the primary motivating factor for how a person conducts themselves, it is referred to as a false self. In order to successfully function in this way it requires a person to either ignore their internal world of feelings, or find a way to not attach them to their source. The resulting distortions in thinking and perceiving can be quite debilitating. This was shown in the treatment of a 40 year old woman who began her contact with a telephone call, asking if I was a doctor who talked to his patients. I replied that I couldn't say, for sometimes I talked, sometimes I said very little, and sometimes I had nothing to say. There was a slight pause before she asked to make an appointment.

In the beginning session, she explained what she meant on the phone and why she decided to see me. She had sought help for a long time and as far as she could tell had gotten nowhere. Now she was desperate, almost at the end of her rope, and was afraid she might once again try to kill herself. She had first looked for help 15 years ago when she felt compelled to engage in sexual affairs while married to her ex-husband. Looking back she could see a similarity in all of the men she was attracted to, including her husband. They all appeared to be extremely confident, powerful, and charismatic, only to turn out to be dominating, intimidating people unable to see beyond their own needs. In many ways they reminded her of her father, with the exception that her father was very frightening to her. He was fanatically obsessed with the bible, distant and completely inaccessible to her. Every communication from him contained some quotation from the bible stating how she should conduct herself. In his presence she was petrified with fear, whereas the men she was drawn to seemed to offer a sense of life and excitement. At the start of each relationship she felt overjoyed, as if she had been rescued from an intolerably isolated existence.

These attachments were like a beacon light to her giving her the only feeling of hope she ever knew. Otherwise she felt completely worthless, overwhelmed by an overpowering fear of humiliation if she expressed anything spontaneous, or withdrawn so completely from all human contact that she became terrified. Subsequently she had married in her late teens to escape both from her family and this unbearable internal state. A few years later she felt equally as trapped in her marriage, which was the onset of her compulsive repetition of the same pattern with other men. Knowing she was in trouble, she instituted a series of psychotherapeutic contacts all of which ended badly. She was left feeling abused and misunderstood, intensifying an already existing feeling of despair. Her initial encounter resulted in a sexual laisson, making her feel desirable and wanted at first; later, however, she felt exploited and betrayed but unable to stop the relationship. She knew it was hurting her but couldn't disengage herself, until she confided in a friend who emphatically insisted that she end it. That was no real answer, for she felt cut off from the outside world, isolated and alone, and became actively suicidal. She then consulted another therapist who she thought was hinting at wanting more than a therapeutic relationship. When she responded in this vein she was rebuffed, and in addition accused of projecting her own wishes while misinterpreting her therapist's motives. It was also at this time that her marriage dissolved, and seeing no way out she made a serious attempt to end her life.

She was hospitalized for a year, during which she conformed to what she sensed the staff wanted of her. She knew she was not revealing any of her trouble, but she felt the time was useful as it forced her to interact with others. It eased her terror of the prospect of pulling away from all interpersonal contact. Following this hospitalization she spent four years with a therapist who dealt with her sexual interest in him by maintaining a firm prohibitive attitude. Her interest was interpreted as a defensive maneuver on her part. She knew his words were true, but thought they were used to keep her at a distance. Often she was speechless so many sessions were spent in total silence, making her feel hopelessly trapped and dependent.

At the same time she continued to be drawn into destructive sexual relationships, each one ending with her feeling hurt, rejected, and filled with shame and self hatred. When she called me she was looking for someone who could help her with her tendency to withdraw and not be silent. My answer had seemed humorous to her, yet she sensed I would take her seriously and respond to questions without throwing them back for her to consider.

In this description there were already suggestions of a very serious disturbance. Much of what occupied her centered around how she had molded herself to match what others wanted in order to make much needed contact. The desperation in her need to establish these connections, as if her life depended upon them, was consistent with this view. The attraction to these sexual unions did not seem to me to be so much an acting out of an unconscious conflict as it was an attempt to shore up a distorted and hence false sense of self. The shattering disillusionments that precipitated her suicidal action sounded to me like a repetition of a severe early trauma.

In these early sessions she was surprised at how freely she was speaking and how much she had to say. She felt as though she didn't have enough time, yet was also worried lest she run out of things to say. She dreaded such a moment and the hopelessness that came with it. It was all too familiar to her. She looked up at me with an unspoken question in her eyes, stating how much she feared there would be no way to get beyond it. I told her she communicated all of the time, whether it was with words or not. Were she to fall silent it would be as powerful a message as any words and we could both discover how well I'd be able to hear her. She looked relieved and shortly thereafter did fall into silence.

I told her what I thought it meant, first focusing on her need to feel held by being heard and understood. This told me a story of how much this was absent while she was growing up. Later she tried to compensate for the effects of not being known, which to me spoke of her having been cut-off from a source of nurturance. Her answer was to seek solace in a series of sexual attachments. Although I didn't have any idea as to why it took this form as yet, it did make me wonder about her experiences with mothering.

My words struck a chord inside of her, initially of surprise. Up to now she had always thought of her difficulty as being primarily with men and a result of the terrible relationship she had with her father. She was so intimidated by him that she considered it to be the most powerful force shaping her life. While I was talking a feeling from the back of her mind became strong enough to notice. She had never been able to put it into words, but it involved her reaction to her mother's "sighs". They expressed her mother's intense disapproval and exasperation.

This was a good example of how the construction of a false self does not necessarily mean that what is true and genuine is either unconscious or otherwise inaccessible. This patient had lived with a feeling in the back of her mind that she was acutely aware of, yet she had not been able to find words for it. When she was receptive, and did not automatically turn away and distract herself, she was able to find some words. Thus the organization of what could be called a false self, which had been her predominant mode of interacting with others, was receding. This made it possible for her true self to come forward.

She went on to elaborate on the feeling. Another part concerned what it was like to be actively excluded from having any thought or feeling of her own. It made her aware of her sensitivity to my every facial expression, as she was searching for any evidence of this attitude on my part. Thinking about it brought up a series of incidents that left her feeling devastated. Throughout her life, in school, work, or social situations, even the slightest hint that she might meet with this kind of disapproval completely immobilized her. She felt ashamed, humiliated, and worthless.

A therapist's task is to establish a properly empathic environment, which enables what is true and genuine to emerge and be expressed. It has to begin with a reliable background formed upon a devotion to whatever is honest, especially in regard to the therapist's functionings. When a false self has had to become firmly entrenched, rather than occupying only a small place in a person's way of adapting, what is genuine and true must be extremely vulnerable to being injured or distorted. Hence it is necessary to be absolutely sure the conditions are safe before it can be revealed. Apparently my welcoming her silence, in combination with my offering her my best understanding of what it signified, provided that element of safety. Her response tended to validate my tentative reading that her mother's influence was a significant factor in her trouble. There was then a movement, reflecting a realignment of the forces within her, towards making her true self accessible. For her to be left in silence was the equivalent of being totally abandoned.

She now began to recall her dreams, which was a new experience for her. At first they were largely static images having little content, no affect, and no associative resonance. Gradually she appeared in the dream imagery, exhibiting a variety of affective states. These, in turn, elicited some associative connections, making her aware of how enraged she had been of the control her mother exerted over her. The experience of being understood was enabling her to show her innate introspective curiosity, something she had kep hidden sometimes even from herself. With it her extreme sensitivity to the emotional nuances taking place in her relationships also was demonstrable. She could see how any move

toward growth or independence, which initially was accompanied
by a feeling of joy and vitality, almost immediately triggered a
powerful self attack. The sense was of her having done something
terribly wrong that would have horrible consequences. I reflected
upon this consistent theme, telling her that it might very well protect her from the dangers she anticipated in being a separate person. I added that I also thought it resulted from having been
traumatized whenever she was assertive or exhibited autonomous
strivings. As I spoke she was silent, but shortly after a host of
memories came to the surface. First they captured the emotional
climate of her childhood, in which girls were treated as worthless
and undeserving and were abused and exploited. This was followed by a series of memories involving sexual invasiveness by her
three brothers. She had to silently endure it, with an inner conviction that she would be shunned, disapproved of, or terribly humiliated if she told anyone. It was as if her brothers had been given
permission to treat her in this fashion. This was her lot in life,
with the only alternative being complete isolation.

With the emergence of her genuine feelings, much that had
either been submerged, shunted aside, or attacked and given no
meaning was now coming more into her awareness. She could
then identify the motives and reasons behind the particular false
self she had constructed in order to enter the world of relationships. She was gaining a better grasp of why she had always used
the avenue of her sexuality as a means of establishing a connection
to others. It had rescued her from the intolerable feeling of being
cut off and abandoned, and from her tendency to withdraw from
all human contact.

She also found words for a lifelong internal impression of her
father that always made her shrink from having anything to do
with him. On the surface she explained it as a fear of his potential
for violence, but underneath she had always sensed how

vulnerable, fragile, and irrational he was. In fact she had been quite protective of him, saving him from being confronted with his weakness whenever it was possible.

I underscored how she had managed to protect valued aspects of herself from the impact of parental insensitivities and prohibitions by withdrawing. Consequently, she felt threatened by the prospect of losing her ability to make attachments. In being cut off from this potential source of help, she was then even more threatened by the strength of her own feelings. The only alternative she could find was to either retreat in despair or to form unhealthy sexual alliances. It did have the temporary effect of making her feel alive and of her having some value.

I had become attuned to how she reacted if there was the slightest lapse on my part. This was a crucial aspect, for her automatic movement was towards molding herself to fit what ever she assumed I either saw or was wishing. Her immediate responses were not very reliable as a source of validation. Early it was hard for me to pick up when I was out of touch with what she was communicating. Now she could see clearly how she reacted to my blindness. Initially it was elaborated by her, silently, to recreate some element of a childhood trauma. In recognizing and telling me what she was doing it became possible for me to correct my mistake, which had a powerful effect upon her. It not only reestablished the empathic qualities of the treatment, but also gave her the experience of being an active participant in that process. She was able to bring out how when she was left in silence by me for too long a time she would feel afraid to complain, much less express the rage she felt building up. She ended up fearing severe criticism if she were to protest and felt dropped. On the other hand if I was too active, even if I was relatively accurate, she would become too concerned with wanting to please me at all costs, even at the expense of bringing what she had to contribute out in the open. She was convinced that if she let me know that my words were beyond what was necessary, it would put me off and I would stop talking altogether. Consequently she would force herself to sit and listen, instead of speaking what she had to say. Whenever she felt intact, full of energy and vitality, and moving forward in her life, concerns would arise that I would expect her to be completely on her own. Therefore she would once again be cut off. If I was off in my understanding, or defensive in my attitude, she would automatically become outwordly conforming and silent. Inwardly she could feel herself trying to mold herself into my view, while seething with anger. It meant a great deal to her when I recognized she had picked up on my failure, which demonstrated to her how much she perceived without realizing it. She had always attributed the inner turmoil she experienced at these moments as evidence of her badness. It helped her to understand the anger that constantly welled up inside and was inexplicable to her. Doors opened to early memories, adding to her increasing insight as to the deprivation she had endured during her formative years.

She had always thought her troubles were the result of growing up in an emotionally depleted environment, as the fifth child of parents who just didn't have enough to go around. It seemed to her like her parents didn't have the emotional resources to meet the needs of their 5 children. Now, however, she could also see the more active and insidiously destructive elements. This was first brought to light in her dreams, which symbolically portrayed the way she was abused and exploited. The very act of recalling dreams was a significant event for her, quite in contrast to the way she previously did everything possible to keep them out of her mind. The value she placed on dreams was in direct proportion to the positive experience she had in grasping their meaning. The associations they elicited were also welcome, as they solidified the new found continuity in her experience.

At one point she dreamed of a table with her family seated around it. There was a very tiny chair next to her mother, leaving no room for her at the table. In the dream she was off to the side seething with anger and envy, while her mother had a satisfied smirk on her face. In another dream a woman, symbolic of her mother, had been presented with three heart-shaped objects. She gratefully received them as she watched my patient feeling hurt and rejected. There was also a dream wherein a religious cult led by an evil couple had a young girl wrapped in a blanket ready to place on a bed of fire. The girl awoke, became aware of her plight, and my patient grabbed her to get her out of danger and placed her in a corner where she wouldn't be found.

All of these dreams gave her a caricatured picture of the emotional attitudes she was surrounded by, and explained to her why her true feelings had to be hidden. It was her way of preserving the core of her being, while presenting a facade to the world. On the surface she appeared unobtrusive, shy, quiet, and ineffectual. This made sense to her, for in that environment she was safer.

During this period she noticed that whenever she did not feel understood by me, she had a reaction reminiscent of being disapproved of by her mother. It would then trigger an active return of the urge to find a sexual partner or plunge her into a pit of despair. She saw how it served to mask a towering rage and a fear of being left if she dared to express it.

Thus in many ways her true and false self were becoming integrated, until she gradually reached a point where she could actually be pleased in becoming angry. With it she discovered a creative, and sarcastic, sense of humor. The joy of being in touch with the world of her emotions made her feel like a whole person. Concurrent with these developments, her aspirations for a career surfaced. She had always considered this kind of independence to be beyond her reach and too frightening to contemplate seriously. She enrolled in school and was excited to find herself capable of learning.

Her ability to recall dreams, the change in the dreams themselves, and the emergence of associative resonance with the dream imagery all reflected the merging together of what had been a true and false self. Along with it she was open to exploring her internal world, leading to early memories bringing meaning to her experiences. Her experience with mothering and the sexual abuse she endured with her brothers were the fertile ground upon which her drive toward destructive sexual laissons were based. When she was held well through being understood she was able to allow her true self to become known.

Probably everyone exhibits a false self in certain situations. Who hasn't answered "fine" when asked how they are today, even though it may be far from a true statement. It can very well be an effective response, as it makes no sense to give a truthful and genuine reply in all circumstances. Nevertheless it would be presenting a false self, and illustrates how describing it as an incomplete self makes it a more accurate and useful concept.

It is quite another matter when a false self is predominant at all times, as a consequence of being cut off from other ways of experiencing and looking at the world. Personality development is intricately interwoven with evolving functions of perception, which are the primary determinants of genuine feeling responses. Intellectual functions, as well as internal thought and language are somewhat later developments. Therefore these more advanced functions will tend to occupy center stage. When growth has been relatively unhampered thoughts and feelings are interwoven and in harmony with each other. One enhancing and enriching the full meaning of the other. If there has been difficulty the world of emotions may be rendered inaccessible to varying degrees, out of which false self configurations are constructed.

Emotions contain the essence of a person's true nature, whereas thoughts can be accessible without continuity to this core. Thus the thinking process can erode a clear view of the underlying emotional world, particularly when pre-verbal traumas are involved. In those situations a false self, though easier to recognize, is much more difficult to integrate. The treatment of a middle aged man demonstrated how a p[reverbal trauma had a life of its own, periodically rising to the surface to surround him. It brought out the erosive, and unyielding nature of the internal attack on anything genuine in his emotional life. Before it was possible for this internal experience to take enough shape to be articulated, however, his defensively organized "false self" had to be relinquished.

The impetus for his calling me was the trouble he was having in a love relationship. At first he was unable to describe what he meant, which was quite striking. In almost everything else he talked about he was quite graphic and articulate. He could only emphasize the fear he had of losing what was an important relationship. The constant criticism he received made no sense to him, so he was left crushed and devastated. In his mind he was sensitive, caring, and devoted all of his attention to meeting this person's needs. Thus he was puzzled. Plans for marriage had been delayed and he was looking for help in understanding what had gone wrong.

He wanted me to know that he was quite knowledgeable about psychological concepts, making him eager to explore what the unconscious meaning of his concern might be. With this in mind he went to great lengths to paint a picture of himself, stressing how kind and considerate he was. However, he was hesitant to be assertive, especially with women. Many examples were given of injustices he had endured at the hands of others, silently absorbing them, while giving an outward appearance of gracious acceptance. This stance had become so ingrained in him that he thought it could cover over some underlying resentment.

This aspect of his personality was quite apparent, for he was consistently obsequious with me. Often he apologized for not having interesting things to say, or for not producing what I might need to understand him better. At this point I had no idea of what was to come, but it was certainly clear that he was actively defended against emotional reactions. A clearly defined, false self was unmistakeable. His attitude was of being a helpless victim of an overpowering authority, which did imply that this was a feature of what he was warding off. The impression he conveyed was of holding back a towering rage that made it impossible to be assertive. His well-fixed character traits seemed designed to protect him from expressing any semblance of aggression. The emphasis he placed upon intellectualizations, together with his ruminative style of thinking, made it evident that a false self was his predominant mode of interacting. It was likely that it also ruled his entire way of thinking.

For a long time the sessions took on a familiar pattern. He would enter the office, settle into a chair, close his eyes, and begin what he called free associating. An incident would come into his mind, usually of some current experience, and he would select an aspect of it that was similar to something in his past continuing on until this thought ran out. After falling silent he would wonder where to go until another idea came to mind, which he followed in the same way. I noticed that whenever I asked a question to clarify something, instead of clarifying it he would nod as if I had introduced a new way of looking at it. He would then approach what he said as if he had gotten off track, and begin a new line of associations.

What was happening gradually became evident to me. He was molding hinself to what he thought I wanted, which appeared to make him feel safe and secure. It looked like he was showing just how his false self operated. I informed him of my thoughts, adding that it must be protecting him from something very disturbing in his emotional life. My words had an amazingly powerful impact. After a silent moment he became visibly upset, and struggled to tell me something that caused a great deal of shame. He could hardly speak, but finally blurted out the words to describe a masturbatory practice he had engaged in for as long as he could remember. He had never spoken of it to anyone, as it seemed strange and he feared revealing it. In order to get aroused he had to give himself an enema, which made him feel sick and disgusted after it was completed. The only time he had any control over the impulse was when he could form an intimate attachment to a woman. It was for this reason that his current difficulty was so upsetting. He was being driven deeper into this auto erotic activity.

This was the first glimmer of something emanating from his hidden, genuine true self, though even here it was hidden in the body of his erotic symptom. I commented to him that it sounded like it made him feel more alive and wondered if it wasn't a way to try and master some as yet unseen trauma that had threatened his very existence. His immediate reaction was to express gratitude for my words. While I was talking he felt relieved and wanted to try and tell me about fragments of mental imagery that periodically flashed into his mind. They were very confusing and his inability to put them into words made him feel he would never be able to communicate them to anyone. He had also known they were important, because he felt so anxious whenever this happened.

This person had utilized his vast intellectual capacities to construct a rigid defensive facade. On the surface it allowed him to attain what looked like an effective, competent mode of functioning. It was a vivid picture of what is meant by a false self. Once this was recognized he could permit internal experiences that tormented him to be expressed. In all likelihood they were linked to infantile emotions. The compulsion he felt to masturbate while being anally stimulated, only relieved by making erotic contact with a woman, suggested that it recreated some early trauma. He had been largely capable of holding his potential for this kind of regression under control, which had dominated during the early months of his treatment. The profound shame accompanying his symptom, and the extreme anxiety associated with vivid, fragmented, and disjointed mental impressions, motivated him to find comfort and security in the only way he knew. This involved molding himself to whatever he felt were my expectations of him.

My recognition of his dilemma and desire to unearth the source of his suffering made him feel safe enough to reveal what he could. An avenue was beginning to open towards the realm of his true self.

He now spent many sessions bringing forth pieces of memory concerning his relationship with his mother, which he could not put together into a coherent picture. In his later childhood she was excessively critical of him, constantly berating and cutting him down. He was viewed by her as clumsy, fragile, and inept, and she consistently called him the bane of her existence. Other fragments of memory were quite different. In these he was brushing her hair being drawn into close, erotically tinged moments of close physical contact. He simply couldn't reconcile these two disparate images. Each time he would begin to describe these recollections, seemingly "out of the blue" his entire body went into spasms, or he winced with a look of abject terror. He had no idea as to what was happening, but he felt like he was being tortured and beaten.

These fragments of true self experience were entering his mind and carried into the communicative field of the treatment. Slowly, isolated fantasies began to appear of being teased at his mother's breast until at the peak of his hungry sucking he was either viciously beaten or thrust into her genitals. There were also brief images of being slammed against a wall accompanied by anguished pleas to stop. He felt pulled into the fantasies, feeling as though they would never end, mobilizing a desperate need to do anything to escape including killing himself. Looking back he realized that these experiences had been plaguing him throughout his life. He had always held a quieter more obscure version of what was now so vivid in the back of his mind. It was precisely at moments when these images pushed forward that he was driven to make contact with a needy woman, or seek solace in his masturbatory symptom. He also recalled feeling suicidal, which seemed strange at the time but made sense now.

Fantasies can be the carrier of emotion or of intellectual activity or sometimes both. When they contain emotional elements they are closer to true self experience. Of course it has to be translated as does all symbolic language. Nevertheless they are an invaluable aid in grasping the significance of the experiences from which they are elaborated. A fantasy cannot develop out of thin air. It is based upon an actual experience and can give important information as to its nature. Apart from how accurate it may, or may not, have been, it can give form and shape to what had been primitive mental impressions. They are representative of true feelings, in contrast to intellectual constructs that have little to contribute in that area.

Gradually a picture of his early life emerged. He had completely blocked out the memory of his mother having been removed from his home for two years when he was age 4. Upon her return she was a changed woman. The critical mother he recalled was from this later period. His recollection of the earlier mother was contained in his fantasies and bodily reactions. They told a story of unpredictable shifts from erotic overstimulation to brutally sadistic attacks. Any outside criticism was like a trigger, activating the bombardment by hostile and erotic stimuli. Since criticism had to be avoided he had created a false self designed to mold himself to whatever he thought others wanted.

The impressions made by these preverbal traumas could only become evident when the conditions were safe. At these moments his advanced levels of functioning (his false self) was relinquished, leaving him immersed in this primitive, chaotic world as alive as when the injuries were inflicted. Afterwards, however, words became available and with it perspective. What had previously been unthinkable was now taking shape. The invasive destructiveness of a sadistic, overstimulating maternal interaction had to be defensively split off, where it operated relatively silently. He had managed to form a means of functioning devoid of a continuous flow of emotions, leading to an instinctually depleted emotionless, and joyless existence. The only fragment of a link to his genuine and true self was contained within his masturbatory symptom.

These two disparate facets of his personality, each in their own way powerful and predominant, were split off from the other. No matter which he was immersed in, it was as though the other did not exist. It was a vivid example of how incomplete his experience was until these two "selves" could be united. Either one was incomplete, yet to refer to them as true and false was helpful in grasping their significance.

Chapter 7

Self Discovery; A Lifetime Journey

I can recall discussing the true meaning of becoming a man with a beloved grandfather. For him it meant taking full responsibility for all of one's actions and behavior, regardless of the reasons, or even whether you were unaware of having had any part at all. It was not an act of blame, nor did it involve pointing a finger at oneself in a critical fashion. Most importantly, taking this kind of responsibility was an opportunity to know and incorporate aspects of oneself that could slip into obscurity. When I finally grasped his message (I was 13 at the time) it seemed like an awesome but overwhelming task. In my mind it required a massive change in perspective, successfully accomplished from that moment forward. This attitude on my part made him laugh, for as he put it, it was an unending approach unlikely to be completed in a lifetime. It did take me a long time to appreciate the wisdom of his words.

Furthermore I have also come to realize that to chase after any elusive or hidden feelings is self defeating, much like swimming upstream. The more you exert will power, the more frustrating and difficult the result. It is only when a person comes to see and appreciate the value of staying quiet and still, so as to be receptive, that feelings previously rendered inaccessible will come forward to be found.

The way in which this shift in attitude can take place was shown in the treatment of a very bright and intellectual 40 year old man who was concerned about an upsetting pattern in his life. He kept moving from one job to another. Sometimes he left in a rage feeling exploited and taken advantage of, while his skills were either ignored or unappreciated. At other times he was fired because he procrastinated on many matters and was considered unreliable. He knew all of this was true, for he could not stand being made a scapegoat and when things were going well he often dragged his feet until others had no choice but to give up on him. He didn't quite know how, but was certain it had to do with how he was brought up. This led him into the details of his childhood years. Although it sounded very painful, he presented it like a story concerning someone else.

His mother was openly psychotic and included her three children, of whom he was the youngest, into her active delusional system. She would spend hours with them preparing for an alien invasion, anticipating their appearance at any moment. Protests were inconceivable, since they would elicit a frightening response; either throwing his mother into a state of panic or precipitating a vicious attack. His father was portrayed as the only sane figure in this chaotic world, so that any contact with him was tremendously overvalued. The picture that emerged, however, was of a man who hid behind his books, largely unavailable to his family, except for occasional moments. The patient had idealized his father and the career he chose grew out of a desire to follow in his father's footsteps. He speculated as to whether his trouble at work was related to his feelings about his father, as though he was afraid to be successful and pass him.

At this point any emotional responses were certainly held in check, but he did hint at the volatility of his emotions whenever he was exploited. Even at this early stage he was exerting a great deal of effort trying to dig out the meaning of his behavior, as well as what was behind his periodic emotional eruptions. The harder he tried, the more distant and intellectualized his reactions became. At the same time he was working hard to present a facade of competence and friendliness, which went against his being receptive to whatever was there.

In succeeding sessions he would become almost "dreamy" when recalling times with his father, underscoring the warmth and affection he felt. He treated me in a similar fashion, referring to how much he looked forward to our time together and how helpful it was to talk about his life. Overtly he sought very little from me, and the distance between us was almost papable to me. It looked as though he could go on endlessly, intellectualizing about his experiences without adding much that was new. Yet he was obviously frustrated in his attempts to get at the source of his trouble. The more frustrated he became, the harder he worked, and the less access he had to how he truly felt.

Occasionally he was quite grandiose in discussing his plans or aspirations. When I commented upon it he laughed as though he was sharing a joke with me about his trying to cover over an underlying feeling of inadequacy. My impression was of his recreating the relationship with his father, on the surface appearing close and involved, but emotionally distant avoiding anything having to do with his pain and suffering. It looked like he clung tenaciously to this position as if his life depended upon it. I thought his grandiosity was a positive sign in that he was at least more spontaneous and less concerned with pursuing his feelings.

His idealization of me was so crucial that he then molded his response to fit what I had said, thus holding me in this lofty position much as he had his father. Although this defensive stance dominated the scene, the evolving alliance between us was becoming stronger.

Gradually inroads were made on his rigid posture, mostly by my calling attention to vague but unspoken feelings of dissatisfaction. He explained it as due to others in his life not hearing him. I wondered if it did not also have to do with my not hearing something, which he immediately denied. However, when I told him of the gap I experienced he was deeply touched. It did make him stop and think. In doing so he noticed how superficial his words were, while sensing the presence of powerful emotions deep inside. They seemed vague but he could feel it having something to do with feeling abandoned by his father. With this statement he burst into sobs, wailing loudly about being alone. The pain he felt was almost unbearable and he struggled to find words that would adequately describe what was rising up. It was like a cloud coming close threatening to engulf and suffocate him, yet at the same time it was firm and unyielding like a steam roller. Talking helped, for in telling it to me he felt connected to someone concerned about him. Slowly it faded away and he looked up appearing relieved.

It was striking to observe how in dropping his defensive attitude he was able to truly listen receptively. An avenue was then open for the very feelings he had struggled to discover to reach him. Initially the form it took was of a deep and painful feeling of abandonment, followed by a primitive mental impression threatening to engulf him. It captured the problem of an immature psyche if there is not enough good self experience to buffer the impact of bodily processes, as well as external insensitivity. It was possible then to speculate that this patient as an infant had met with destructive mothering. The emergence of the enveloping cloud, although necessitating a need for defense, reflected his new found capacity to represent the unseen and unknown. The process of self discovery was now well on its way. First he had to see how his frantic efforts to dig into the depths only served to insure they would remain untouched. Only then could he be open and receptive. Nothing fosters the process of self discovery more than a welcoming attitude, especially towards whatever emerges spontaneously. Fantasied imagery is particularly useful, because it has been less exposed to more advanced psychic functions. Consequently it is closer to the earlier developmental experiences that have had the greatest impact, and thus have had to be rendered inaccessible.

The mind is built up on mental representations, which then form the foundation for all psychological functions to evolve. The underlying imagery is exposed to processes of depersonification, creating thought patterns that are hard to link to their origins. It is for this reason that mental contents like fantasies (and dreams as well) have a greater potential for revealing the full and true meaning of a given experience.

Memories, based upon actual experience, could be likened to a photograph. They show something, seemingly undeniable, but often mistakenly required before an event is considered to be real. Mistakenly since a photograph can hide the subtleties, just as a memory can only give an incomplete picture. A caricature, on the other hand, brings out nuances that are hidden through exaggeration and elaboration. In this sense they may play a bigger role in exposing the truth, much in the manner of fantasies. To cast them aside as insignificant, unimportant, and worse as unreal, is like discarding the most valuable component.

In gaining an appreciation of this attribute of fantasies a person's attitude can shift, so that they will be examined more closely for their meaning. If the question was asked as to which was more real, a photograph or a caricature, what answer would be correct? Obviously the answer would depend greatly on the circumstances. In some ways it is the photograph; in other ways the caricature. A complete picture would depend upon both. Often the memory is what is hidden, while the fantasy can be received to provide a pathway to integrate the two. Fantasies are thus a vital element in the journey towards self discovery.

Who hasn't heard the phrase, "That's just your imagination", meant to diminish their importance. I know many children who when they hear such a comment feel the urge to protest, yet are quiet since it is confusing. The fact that it is their imagination is indisputable, but the protest is against the implication that because it's their imagination it isn't either real or credible. In fact it may be precisely due to it's being their imagination that makes it both real and credible.

In addition, imagination is an essential ingredient necessary to keep the younger aspects of an individual vibrant and alive. It reminds us that one is never too young to begin the journey and never too old to complete it. A 3 year old child illustrated how much can be accomplished at a very young age, and how vital fantasies are for widening the field of awareness. She was referred after she had been complaining for several months of severe stomach aches and occasional episodes of vomiting with no apparent physical reason. Her parents were quite psychologically minded and thought she was upset about her mother's pregnancy, anticipating she would be displaced by the new baby's presence. When they first told her about the pregnancy she had seemed pleased, and began to pretend that she too, like her mother, was pregnant. Initially they had seen it as cute, but as time went on and she appeared to believe she actually did have a baby inside of her they started to worry. She also got more upset by it and they were at a loss as to how to comfort or reassure her. She had asked to see a doctor and so they called me.

Immediately upon entering my office she started to talk, obviously under great pressure to get everything said. She walked in, looking very poised and proud, took off her coat and placed it on a chair, as if she were underscoring her ability to be self sufficient. Then, in a very serious and emphatic way, she informed me that she knew she had a baby in her tummy. The only possible way it could come out was through her mouth. She had thought and thought about it, but hadn't as yet figured out how to do it. That's why she came to see me. I was a doctor and she hoped I would know a way to help her get it out.

This was obviously a powerful fantasy that occupied her mind and that she experienced as being deeply embedded within her body. It underscored how the mind is a part of the body, though what it was meant to express was at this point not at all clear. Of course there were many hints as to what might be involved, but jumping to conclusions is never a wise course to take.

She went on to say that she had tried to force it out, to the extent that she threw up. This was no answer for it made her tummy hurt worse. Pausing for a moment she asked if I believed that there really was a baby inside of her. This was an interesting question, because it implied that in her mind I might not. It suggested to me that she must have encountered such an attitude often and was probing to see if it also applied to me. I answered by asking her why it was a question, since so far she hadn't given me any indication that I shouldn't. She then explained that everyone she met thought she made it all up. Her parents had tried to tell her how babies are made and born and how it was impossible for a baby to really be there. They just didn't think there was one and worse they didn't know how to get it out. Her tears welled up as she described what hurt so much. It wasn't a part of her, which made it scary, since it could grow bigger and even eat her up. Now her fantasy was being elaborated. It was something both foreign yet attached to her. She thought of it as getting bigger and consuming her. Listening I thought how it really was doing all of that. Rather than being an integrated and incorporated part of herself it was attacking her and hence foreign. She, in turn, was getting smaller, as it occupied more of her time and energy. The world around her was responding to her fantasy with a lack of appreciation for how real the fantasy was in what was expressed.

She then looked up at me and asked if I had any idea of how to do it. The anguish in her voice cried out for help. I told her that since she was convinced it had to come out of her mouth, I thought it was an important clue. We would have to figure out together just what that meant. She immediately caught on to my words and was intrigued by the ideas. She listed all the things she could think of that came out of her mouth; food, spitting, vomiting.....and suddenly her eyes lit up ......words! We both laughed and I remarked that she had found something that felt right. She thought so too and got very excited; paused, and a puzzled look crossed her face. I said that she had shown me how much she wanted to do things herself, but this looked like she might need my help for it wasn't just any words. We had to find the words that fit, so they could bring the baby out. She nodded her head vigorously yes, appearing relieved. We agreed to keep meeting until we had found those words.

This very young child's basic sense of trust was quite evident in the way she approached her contact with me. She sought to be understood, expected that she would be, and was confident that I would try to help. Her concern was almost totally centered on getting relief from her inner torment. By implication she had an abundance of good self experience. Her symbolic functions were well developed, enabling her to use them in both expressing and disguising wishes and feelings that were too disturbing to experience. There were certainly many reasons for her fantasy to take the form of a baby growing inside, undoubtedly shaped by whatever was aroused by her mother's pregnancy. The anticipated loss of her place in the sun, her anger and fear of rejection, a wish to identify with and be close to her mother, and perhaps a precocious, budding rivalry were among the possibilities.

My interventions were especially facilitating when they acknowledged her independent strivings. At the same time they addressed her hunger to be nurtured. Simply by being able to talk freely, knowing that I truly believed in the reality of fantasies and what they had to offer, she came upon the striking idea that it was words that needed to be spoken for the baby to be delivered. She then could feel the potential to reach the unspoken truths that she had harbored inside. There were two kinds of reality. The reality of the fantasy taking the form of a baby, and the reality of talking in the form of the right words to deliver it. The proper words were not as yet identified, but a clear direction had been established. My task was not so much to give her the words as it was to provide an opportunity for them to emerge.

In succeeding sessions she was eager to talk. First she wanted to clear up the confusion in her mind as to how babies were made. She couldn't quite grasp what it meant that her daddy had put a seed into her mommy where it met an egg and grew into a baby in a special place. This made her think that somehow she must have swallowed one of his seeds, and she didn't want the baby. These last words were spoken with such force that she was taken by surprise.

A clearer picture was now coming out as to what lay at the root of her trouble. The confusion was created by an interweaving of the two forms of reality; her fantasies about how babies are made and born, interspersed with the pieces of reality provided by her parents. At the moment that she uttered the words proclaiming how she did not want a baby, I thought we were pretty close to finding the right words.

I then commented upon the angry sound in her voice and she launched into a tirade concerning all the changes taking place in her life. Her mother was always too tired to play with her, everyone was excited about the pregnancy, and she hated it. For several sessions she spent the entire time venting her anger. Sometimes she was so furious her face got red as though she could barely contain it. However, there were other times when she expressed it playfully, imagining how she could make her mother and father be as hurt as she was. Through all of this there was no mention whatsoever of the baby inside of her. At this point our appointments were interrupted by the new baby's arrival. She returned looking subdued and hesitant and in a barely audible voice mumbled that she supposed that I wanted to hear about her baby sister. I wondered if she was expressing some concern as to whether I was interested in her, but before I could go on she burst forth with incidents centering around her reactions to the baby. This theme was predominant, particularly emphsizing what it was like to watch her nursing. At one point I alluded to her wish to be a baby, which made her stop, nod her head yes, and after a pause change it to an emphatic no. She then smiled, reveling in how good it felt to be bigger. Almost as an after thought, she casually stated that the baby inside of her was gone. With a pensive look, and like she was recalling something from long ago, she began to tell me what was so awful for her before the baby was born. Everytime she saw her mother's tummy get bigger it gave her a sick feeling inside. It was the idea of her mother and father doing something without her knowledge and away from her, and this was the result. She just couldn't stand this constant reminder. Whenever it came to mind the only way she could ease it was to imagine her daddy making a new baby with her.

It had appeared that expressing the anger evoked by the impending arrival of a new baby was the major factor in her being able to deliver the baby. Now, however, I thought she was bringing out the deeper motive for that particular symptom. Once she was able to express her hostility, though not openly evident while it was happening, the baby inside was being delivered with her angry words. Her casual reference to the disappearance of the symptom was interesting, for she was treating it as if it were not noteworthy. In a sense this attitude was quite fitting, for in giving up the symptom more of what it was designed to defend against came to the surface. She not only had to swallow her aggressive feelings (the seed), but she was also holding the more threatening fantasies out of her awareness (the growing baby). Her greatest anxiety involved her parents engaged in hidden activities, having sexual overtones, and from which she was excluded. The implied betrayal, as well as the overstimulation and curiosity, added to the threat. Although her initial anxiety was temporarily relieved by imagining her father making a baby with her, it became a source of even greater trouble. In a sense she was now delivering the afterbirth.

This child's treatment was somewhat unusual in two respects. First, her symptom was an amalgam of healthy and pathological forces on a solid and intact structural foundation. Second, she had an exceptional ability to express herself verbally at a very young age. Nevertheless some important principles were highlighted. Especially noteworthy was the function of fantasy in mental activity. Arguments as to whether a given event was real or imagined then fade into the background, as the question of what story each has to tell moves into prominence. With it stress is placed upon the role of fantasy in gaining a deeper appreciation of what is real.

Chapter 8

Who is the Authority

A uthority is an interesting word. Originally it came from the word author, which means to cause to grow or to increase. It refers to one who creates, produces, or brings something into being. This simple piece of knowledge identifies the wonder of authority; that is, to be the one who fosters growth and learns. In that context being your own authority is the only one that counts, and should not be given up to another.

Certainly others can be in positions of power and command, but if they are used properly they can only enhance ones authority. In this sense the only person with warranted authority is the individual him or herself. The extent of it is defined by the degree of knowledge that one possesses. Thus warranted authority signifies that the individual is the author.

Unfortunately the outside world, and sometimes the person concerned, may frequently grant authority to those who are in no position to use it well. In that case the authority is unwarranted, and if or when it is accepted trouble arises. (For example, the world gives me the authority to perform surgery. If I accepted that it would be a disaster.) In those instances where unwarranted authority is accepted, it is most likely a compensatory reaching for the genuine authority that is missing.

There is a saying that made me smile when I first saw it. I do not know what the author of it may have meant, but I can describe what it said to me. The message suggested that a person should not blindly follow rules presented to them by others, no matter that the rules may have been constructive or useful to whoever made them. It is essential for a person to find their own unique guidelines. This does not mean, however, that others rules should be ignored, rebelled against, or in any way disregarded. That attitude alone would work against learning and growth. The task would be to give them serious consideration, decide to retain what may or may not be applicable or helpful, and eliminate those that serve no useful purpose. It is akin to the way our digestive system functions in absorbing what is nurturing, and eliminating what is either of no use or toxic. The saying was, "Sacred cows make great hamburgers".

Children are often told that they are to obey people in authority, regardless of the circumstances and with no consideration as to whether their authority is warranted. Of course there is, in most instances, a kernel of truth in the idea that those in authority possess better judgement or have a broader perspective on what is required (similar to the sacred cows). There may be a good reason to take such an approach at times. Unfortunately, however, too frequently it is not balanced by helping a child determine and select what is constructive and growth promoting and what is detrimental. It is one thing to follow a rule with the clear awareness of its absurdity, quite another to believe in its value. Almost all children intuitively know the validity of these considerations, though they may or may not have the words to describe it. This is particularly true of younger children, the very ones I hear people refer to as not old enough to understand such concepts. Strikingly those very same children may so internalize the prohibitions against questioning authority, that when they get older their awareness seemingly is inaccessible. When this occurs their protest may only be able to be expressed in hidden ways not even recognized by the themselves.

The treatment of a 7 year old girl demonstrated how much these kinds of prohibitions can dominate a child's life. This aspect of her difficulty was not openly in evidence at the outset, though it could have been inferred from her behavior. She was originally referred because of her parents concern about her extreme tension and unhappiness. They had tried for some time to talk her into seeing a psychiatrist, but she had always resisted. Her teacher was also worried about her poor performance in spite of what looked like greater potentials. She was extremely bright, yet unable to do well, and frustrated whenever she faced anything new and unfamiliar. Her parents described her as driven and perfectionistic, constantly over striving and under achieving. A feeling of tension filled the air whenever they were with her. The slightest obstacle would end up in any angry outburst, or in berating herself and saying she wished she were dead. When she developed an eye tic they no longer listened to her objections and insisted she have psychological help. Although she fought with her parents about coming to see me, she did reluctantly comply when they stood firm.

I had not as yet seen this child, but I could already make some assumptions about the role that rules, regulations, and respect for authority played in her life. On the surface her parents were warm, sensitive, and caring, yet in many subtle ways were bound by rules themselves. Consequently almost every corner of her life was filled with implied or explicit demands, expectations, and unspoken concerns that her behavior cast a bad light upon them as parents. Thus she lived in an environment with very little room for anything that might go against what the "authorities" considered appropriate.

She came to her first appointment looking prim and proper, picked out a chair and sat immobile as she talked. She spoke in an overly mature fashion about herself, her relationship with her parents, sister, and friends, and her involvement in school and outside activities. Periodically she displayed an eye blinking tic, to which she was seemingly oblivious. She worked very hard to present a picture of herself as a competent, adequate little girl, who was perfectly content with her life. As I listened to her my impression was of a tightly wound spring, so I eventually expressed this to her. She responded by starting to giggle and said, "that's silly. People can't be like springs". She added that she thought I was awfully weird.

Her reaction made me think I had made an empathic connection to some inner longing that she had to hold tightly in check. It certainly looked promising that she felt able to challenge my words, and there was a relieved and playful quality in the way that sie did it.

At the end of the session I told her that I thought she had given me a picture of her outside appearance, but it might be good to meet regularly in order to learn what was going on inside of her. Once more she giggled, stating that I was being silly again. All that people had inside of them was a heart and lungs. Now her whole demeanor relazed, her movements were more spontaneous, and she eagerly agreed to the idea of regular appointments.

Although she was trying to look competent, the defensive qualities of her attitude stood out. It was evident in the rigidity of her posture, the overcontrolled tone in her voice,and the careful way she chose words. In addition her attention was focused almost exclusively upon immediate perceptions and logical kinds of thoughts. There was at least no overt sign of spontaneity, or of allowing fantasies to enter her mind, as though everything had to be organized. This kind of adaptation could have many possible meanings, but one had to do with how constricted she was by prohibitions she had internalized. My early metaphorical comment concerning her tense appearance and later around being introspective were taken literally and rejected. Yet her giggling and mildly playful rebuke suggested to me that they also gave her some feeling of being understood, as well as permission to be herself. The change in her behavior at the end gave some indication that she felt safe enough to continue in this direction.

Following this initial session she looked forward to coming and was enthusiastic in greeting me. Her movements and verbal expressions were increasingly less constricted and she was full of vitality. Her overly mature facade dissolved as she exhibited a wide range of emotional reactions. At first these centered around her dislike and envy of a number of children, followed by her graphic emphasis on the intensity of her hatred of school. It was the effort and concentration that the teachers demanded that was the worst, and especially their authoritarian attitude. More than anything she longed to just sit in front of the t.v. and watch cartoons, free of any expectations of any kind. In her eyes teachers were a source of pressure and she visualized them silently looking at her in disapproving ways. It was as though her every move was violating whatever they wanted her to do. Immediately then she began to talk about her concern over children who were out of control, which led them into dangerous positions.

Encouraged by the conditions of the treatment she was obviously becoming more spontaneous, but at the same time more frightened of the forces mobilized inside of her that were pushing to be expressed. Her reference to the disapproving teachers, and children out control, sounded like a reflection of how dangerous she felt her own impulses and feeling were. It pointed to one of the reasons she had taken in the prohibitions of the outside world, as they gave her a way of managing them. It also sheds light on how this kind of solution often occurs in a parental environment that depends upon rules and regulations, in place of finding what is right, to establish what is best. A child is then missing the opportunity to learn what is right and best from within. This approach requires a background of firm discipline, along with a willingness to assess a child's input, in coming to meaningful decisions. Children then can regulate the power and strength of their own feelings. This child's need for prohibitions required that they be quite harsh, creating a problem of their own. She was clearly at war with herself.

Periodically she would turn to me for nurturance and comfort, as she sought relief from this inner state of turmoil and conflict. On one occasion, for example, she was telling me how hard it was to fall asleep. She felt restless and frustrated, "like having an itch you couldn't scratch because you couldn't reach it". It reminded her of the movie, "Lord of the Flies". The more she thought of it the more uneasy she felt, as it was too scary to think of situations with no rules. She wondered if I couldn't give her something to make her feel better and safe. I told her that I thought the experience she was having with me, where I was encouraging her to express whatever was on her mind, was making her feel overwhelmed. At the same time I thought she felt this was terribly forbidden, all of which created a battle inside of her. It looked to me like she wanted me to give her some kind of rule to follow that would put her at ease. Her immediate response was to wish she could be just like her father. He always seemed to have an answer to every problem.

This child's wish to have relief from the impact of powerful feelings and the punitive restraints they evoked led her to turn to me for comfort and protection. It also mobilized a wish to possess her father's confidence, which I thought contained some mixed feelings, partly to be thumbing her nose at me as if to say I was a know-it-all. I considered it a positive movement on her part and a sign that she was more in touch with the realization that she was truly the author of her own feelings. The harsh prohibitions that had so restricted her were lessening their hold on her, as she felt freer in expressing herself.

The follwing session occured shortly afterwards. She began by telling me how much she knew and how capable she was. She had brought a book to demonstrate how well she could read. In addition she wrote out some complicated words to show me how good she was at spelling. In doing so it was evident that she both misspelled and misread several words. Her attitude was emphatically self righteous, as she challenged me to try and find any mistakes. I said she seemed to be questioning whether I would tell her things I could see were wrong and help her to face her own uncertainty. At first she got angry, proclaiming she was right and she knew it. She put the book down to show her skill at doing gymnastic tricks, wanting to be sure that I realized how much more adept she was than her older sister. Suddenly she became embarrassed and speaking softly referred to her envy and admiration of her sister. With great hesitation she admitted that she was always fighting hard to outdo her but was never successful. She was driven to show everyone that she could do everything well. When she couldn't it made her feel frustrated and she began to hate herself. The envy of others abilities had actively come to the surface after having been hidden behind her constant striving for perfection..

Following a pause her attitude toward me shifted and she teasingly asked if I could do the gymnastic moves that she had done. She did some more, each time commenting on how impossible it would be for me to repeat them. She thought I was much too clumsy and awkward and was convinced that I must feel very envious of her. She went onto say that she knew I was disappointed in myself as I watched her and was wishing I could be more agile. I simply noted out loud how she was now attributing feelings to me that she herself had experienced shortly before. Perhaps it was because they were so painful to her. I added that I also thought it was a way getting me to know what it felt like to her. It was like she didn't feel complete, and was disappointed in me when I wasn't able to help her see where that feeling came from.

Being able to use me as a figure to whom she could attribute her own feelings aided her in seeing them more clearly. It was then unclouded by the humiliation, and extreme feelings of failure that accompanied her envy. I was also introducing a new idea to her; that she harbored these feelings for a reason. Furthermore that was not yet visible to either her or me, while underscoring how the answers resided within her. I had taken an overall view of what was so trouble some to her and played it back, so she could have something to react to. In this way I was trying to find a pathway that could lead her to the source of her concern. Underneath it all, for some as yet unseen reason, she did not feel like a complete person.

She suddenly remembered a dream; in it she was in a bedroom with her parents. A monster was trying to break into the room and she just had to protect her mother. Her father had disappeared but she knew he was okay. The dream made her think of how much she missed her mother after school. She fantasied sitting on her mother's lap watching t.v. Again in a soft voice she spoke of feeling disappointed in her mother, becoming somewhat contemptuous as she described her mother's ineptness. I commented on how she had seen me in a similar way, which I thought protected her from another feeling she had about me that reminded me of the monster in her dream.

The fact that my words about her feeling incomplete served to evoke a dream, made me feel I was on the right track. She had listened attentively and what emerged was psychic content (the dream) that was closer to hidden aspects of herself. Following the dream she skipped over the anxiety arousing monster threatening to break onto the room, to focus on protecting her mother. This led her to imagine close comforting contact with her, and then to feeling contempt for her ineptness. The dream monster practically shouted out that it represented her own feelings, in that it posed no threat to her only to her mother. She had expressed the same feeling of contempt toward me. This is what made me think that as difficult as it was it may have been safer for her than other feelings, symbolized by the monster, that may also have been present. In my playing this idea back to her I was showing her how I listened, what I heard, and how it could only be useful if it brought forward what she needed to hear from within herself. It is therefore the patient's authority that ultimately guides the way.

Her attitude became very secretive, as she told me she was thinking about alot of things but they were very embarrassing. She didn't know if she could say them out loud. Slowly she revealed her fantasies concerning sexual activities, interspersed with comments about the bad words she was thinking and using. She recalled giggling with her friends as they used bad words and noticed how exciting it was. This led her to elaborating upon her wish to have a boy friend, and to her interest in a boy she knew. She stopped, felt embarrassed again, and alluded to her curiosity about male genitals.

Now a clearer picture was emerging in regard to the nature of the conflicts she was struggling with. There was an intense disappointment in, and rivalry with, her mother. It alternated with envy and contempt in relation to her mother's special position. Her envious feelings about her mother's greater abilities were displaced first onto her sister and later came to life in the relationship with me. These feelings were barely disguising the closeness and intimacy she longed for with her mother. When the defensive nature of these struggles was addressed, more threatening sexual fantasies, impulses, thoughts, and ideas began to emerge. The appearance of these underlying feelings was indicative of her no longer having to maintain such a rigid defensive posture. One consequence was of a greater degree of access, and hence more interplay, between what was conscious, preconscious, and unconscious in her internal world. This greater amount of freedom from the need for prohibitions allows what is infantile and hidden to be exposed to more advanced integrative functions. In this fashion her self knowledge and awareness was expanding.

It was now apparent to her that her confidence was growing, which was consistent with the changes that were taking place. Confidence basically refers to one's ability to confide in oneself, usually manifested by a feeling of being solid and secure. Having a pathway open to confide in oneself is indicative of a harmonious flow of activity between all sectors of the personality. In such a position there is no question as to who is the authority. The person is the author of their choices, decisions, behavior, and feelings. There is no need to attack or undermine any aspect of oneself, only a need to see or understand what has been in the dark.

Chapter 9

Non-Verbal Communication and the Power of Words

It is interesting that we rely so much on verbal communications, when they often are the least reliable. Conversely there is a tendency to either ignore, or not give much validity to the idea that we communicate strong and meaningful messages in our gestures, bodily movements, and entire manner of conducting ourselves; all without words. The phrase "body language" reflects an awareness of this element in human communication, though its interpretation has to depend heavily upon words. The interpreter cannot help but give a reading influenced greatly by subjective reactions, which adds to the difficulty. The interpretation tends to say more about the interpreter than what is being expressed, which is one reason so much emphasis is placed upon words. They do enable us to at least have the illusion of being understood, yet whether we are or are not is another matter.

The assumption is often made that two people speaking the same language are acquainted with words that will have the same meaning to both. Unfortunately this may not always be the case. Body language, by contrast, is clearly unique and cannot be fully understood until it is translated into words. For that reason whatever words are used have extreme value, as long as their limitations are recognized. Appreciating these complexities in human communication is vital, for along with it is the realization of how much each of us has to learn from the other. What a difference that can make in our listening posture, as there is an automatic shift into wondering how the other person's words could be right. It is far too easy to introduce adversarial qualities into a relationship by immediately assuming one's view has the greater degree of clarity. There is no other choice when this occurs than to hear the others productions as inaccurate, defensive, or in some other way distorted.

The effort directed towards discovering whatever is true in another's words is amply rewarded, for the field of vision is then expanded for both parties. In addition the process itself will be unearthing important clues towards grasping non-verbal body language communications in particular. One example was seen with an 8 year old girl, who was referred due to her consistent underachievement in school.

She was eager to come to her sessions and wanted to talk about her trouble. Mostly this centered around an almost constant feeling of frustration and boredom, as well as what she called "growing pains". These were pains everywhere in her body, which felt to her like something was trapped inside and trying to grow.

Right from the start she was indicating that body language was a significant feature in how she communicated. Furthermore she did have some words to apply to what was hurting her. Yet she was frustrated as her inability to say more about it, as if she knew there was alot to be said.

In the early months she complained of her pains incessantly, becoming increasingly irritable and upset as she did. She was totally convinced that I didn't believe her and was silently laughing at her. There was nothing I could do or say to alter her conviction and it was terribly disturbing to her. The tenacity of this fixed belief made her feel certain that she could not be understood.

This child was placing the entire focus of her attention on somewhat vague body sensations. Any attempt I made to try and shed light on the meaning of her reaction only made her more irritable and solidified the position she held. She was clinging to what she knew, although she suffered alot in doing so. She simply refused to consider anything that was unknown to her. It was clear that I had to find some way to diminish her need for such an unyielding defensive reaction, before the underlying source of this anxiety could be revealed. Her behavior cried out that in some way whatever I was either doing, or not doing, was bad for her. This made it essential for me to locate, if I could, what was making this impression. My first consideration was that I might unwittingly be functioning in some depriving, overstimulating, or impinging manner, or that in some unrecognized way I was distant and defensive. After exploring her words and my responses, it did not seem to me to be the case. There was no indication from her that I possessed any of these attributes, instead emphasis was that it made no difference what I did. It implied that I was experienced this way as a result of her attitude. Nevertheless I still felt some important communication was not being understood by me.

With this in mind. I considered how she might be correct. First I noted how she was preoccupied with disturbing bodily sensations, accompanied by a constant anticipation of being humiliated. By implication it suggested that there was extreme opposition to identifying the specific bodily urges That might be involved. This led me to think of how hidden erotic, infantile feelings might be expressed this way. I then recalled that her greatest concern was that I couldn't understand, at which point it struck me that she was quite accurate in that perception. Were such feelings implicated in this hidden language of her body, I had in no way addressed it as an important communication.

Taking all of these ideas into account I told her she was right in her conviction that I didn't believe her. I went on to say that I had not spoken at all of the kind of messages her body might be expressing, and hiding, in the pain she had described. I could see that if I was unable to translate this language for her she would remain trapped. Her response was immediate and filled with excitement. She talked about exploring caves, forests, and jungles, placing special emphasis upon the thrills and dangers she could meet. She imagined entering a dark cave, unable to see, but wanting to go deeper inside excited by the prospect of what she could find. The same theme was portrayed as she imagined going through dark forests or jungles having to push aside underbrush to explore further. Her entire demeanor became lively as she speculated on the possibilities of what she might discover.

My realization, and perhaps more important the shift in my attitude as I listened to how she was right, struck a responsive chord in her. All of the fantasies that poured forth from her, along with her unbridled excitement, stood in contrast to her previous unhappy demeanor. This was quite evocative to me, something I had not experienced with her as I felt lost and unable to see a helpful direction to take. Now her fantasies sounded to me like they were symbolic of her relationship to her own body, expressing a desire to explore it freely. I thought she was telling me how much she needed my help in order to move in that direction.

I then said to her that I thought she was calling my attention to her strong urge to explore her body, and especially its inner parts. Her reaction was striking. She lay down on the couch, became very subdued while openly rubbing her genitals. Talking softly she referred to my words giving her permission to do what she wanted to do ever since she first began to see me. She felt blocked whenever she tried to talk and had always known that the only way to get past it was to masturbate. When she did, words came easily.

I realized that at the outset, when she put so much emphasis on her body sensations (calling them "growing pains"), I had briefly considered something akin to what she was talking about now. However, it was much too obscure in my mind to know how to talk with her about it. Her irritability looked to me like she anticipated that these kinds of instinctual urges would be exposed prematurely. Without realizing it I had been reluctant to address this conflict directly, worried that it would intensify her defensive posture and entrap her even more. When I finally came to speak about it I stressed how I had held all this back. Her need to be so protective immediately diminished. What emerged were thinly disguised masturbatory wishes, expressed through fantasies of exploring caves, forests, and jungles. In my articulating what that might mean she felt relieved enough to openly masturbate while describing what it accomplished for her. Prior to this just my adult presence resonated so strongly with her infantile prohibitions that she could not allow any movement. It was in this way that she felt trapped. Unbeknownst to me it was vital to her that I recognize her dilemma before she could feel safe enough to expose her vivid fantasy life. Accompanying this development was a change in her attitude towards the unknown, from one of extreme conflict and anxiety to one of excitement and challenge. From a dangerous undertaking it had become a liberating journey.

The fantasies themselves contained the idea of looking deeper inside, to find new and eagerly anticipated experiences. This captured the significance of having access to her hidden feelings, and how they provided vitality as they enabled her to grow. The fact that her defenses were so stringent that they prevented forward movement, together with so much attention directed to her bodily sensations, gave notice that the greatest danger centered around linking her fantasy life to those sensations. This is what masturbating did for her. It allowed her to experience genital sensations devoid of fantasy, just as the fantasy allowed an unseen figure to be sought after with a sense of excitement. In connecting the two there was danger, which her defensive attitude prevented.

In succeeding sessions, evidence of this connection being made showed itself. She spoke about a wild cousin, going into detailed descriptions of the sexual games they played in exploring each other's bodies. She recalled passing a toll booth on the highway unable to see who was inside, and then imagining it was a man who looked like her cousin. These kinds of fantasies frightened her. Her thoughts shifted to a longing to be close to her mother, yet not wanting to cling to her. Her parents were divorced when she was 3 years old and she missed her father alot. However, she also recalled visits with her father that at times were frightening, for she always felt the pull to return to her mother when she was with him.

The nature of the conflict and the source of her anxiety were now more apparent. This was the step she was unable to take before, since the strength of her defenses prevented the connections she was making. "Growing pains" described her situation very well, for she could feel the underlying push toward growth being held back and causing her pain. The fantasy expressed in the play with her cousin was somewhat readily allowed, whereas the fantasy of an unseen man continued to cause anxiety. The danger of linking these kinds of feelings to her father was just coming into view, which triggered a regressive return to an earlier struggle. This concerned her extreme dependency upon her mother and wish to be free of its crippling effects. In finding the proper words that captured her feelings the trouble no longer had to be expressed through the language of her body. Accurate words had provided her a pathway to anchor her experiences in her mind, where they could be exposed to her more advanced integrative functions. In being liberated from her body sensations her growth could then continue.

Preverbal experiences, mental impressions that have not yet been verbalized, and overly intense traumatic feelings that have had to be deflected into bodily processes need meaningful words to surround them, if clarity is to be attained. Often a word may be found that feels just right. The conscious intent in selecting the word may reside in one direction, whereas the root meaning of the word may point to an entirely different significance. The disparity between the two can be quite revealing, capturing an unrecognized and deeper truth. The right word that is then used can be helpful in solidifying a firmer grasp upon self awareness and knowledge.

At one time I had regarded using a dictionary as a chore, until I was introduced to the rich store of information that it contained. Originally my only acquaintance with it was distated by some demand to find a definition, or at times having some mild curiosity about the meaning of a word I didn't recognize. All in all it seemed a dry and lifeless exercise, and one I usually avoided. Once I discovered the treasures it held by directing my attention to the root meaning of words, I became acutely aware of how the original usage had either been changed or altered in a pattern that was clearly not accidental. Placing the modification side by side with its source opened up an entirely new way of understanding the value of words. Dimensions of meaning emerged that I had only dimly suspected.

I could recall moments when I was referred to as weird, because I was doing something that went counter to what was considered normal. At the time it sounded like I was being criticized or put down, yet what I was doing felt right to me. Nevertheless the word seemed appropriate, though I couldn't explain the vague sense that both things were somehow correct. On the surface it was certainly contradictory, for I also thought of people as weird when their behavior was unusual. The dictionary made clear what I was reacting to, allowing me to gain a sharper focus and broader perspective.

It was a revelation to find that the root meaning of the word weird was to in essence follow one's own destiny. I could then see the significance of my response with a greater clarity. After that it made me smile whenever I was called weird, for it was a comment upon my unique style of expressing myself. I was following my own destiny. Whatever the negative implications were, they no longer struck me as being hurtful. It also made me realize that in making such judgements a vulnerable, sensitive place in that person must have been touched. A whole new world of meaning emerged, as I noticed the choices people made of emotionally laden words. They unearthed a gold mine of enlightenment.

I thought of occasions in which I had done something that was labelled not nice and though I knew I was being criticized the word didn't seem to fit. Conversely there were times I was judged to be nice, yet I knew I was being polite but didn't think of it as being particularly nice. Once again the dictionary cleared up my confusion. The root of the word nice means ignorant and unknowing, making the word fit both situations perfectly. I was deemed not nice when I persisted in noticing implicit, emotional nuances that were supposed to be ignored. On the other hand I was viewed as nice when in my politeness I overlooked these same attitudes.

Listening to words with this perspective has been illuminating, and highlights the power of words. Subsequently I heard the old saying, "sticks and stones can break my bones, but names can never hurt me", in an entirely different way. Words can inflict a great deal of hurt, more so than the bruises of sticks and stones. They can linger on and the hurt does not heal quickly. In addition they can add to a person's already existing doubts as a result of which the hurt persists. In all probability an intuitive knowledge of this attribute is behind the saying, trying to construct a barrier against this detrimental property of hurtful words. Verbal attacks can indeed exploit the feelings of inadequacy almost all people possess to some degree. Through pinpointing an individual's area of greatest vulnerability, usually containing a partial truth, the words can't be ignored or cast aside. The meaning they tap into may be distorted or obscured by the hostile manner in which they are spoken. However, they are generally taken to heart due to their closeness to some unspoken but disturbing piece of self knowledge. It is sad when the only available alternative is the one conveyed in the saying. The solution is one that tries to deny the power of words. It stresses an approach that encourages closure as a means of protection, which narrows the range and depth of human experience. How much better to remain open to the world, with the whole gamut of feelings that this entails. The question then becomes how to absorb hurt while gaining perspective. The end result is in broadening one's understanding of oneself as well as of others.

I have found it to be a mind expanding experience to learn the root meaning of words, particularly those that are applicable to a person's daily life or emotional state. Whether one is the perpetrator or target of verbal abuse, nothing is really added to new learning. However, finding a way to grasp the underlying meaning can go far in that direction. Who hasn't had their feelings hurt at one time or another by being called stupid, and protested loudly that it isn't true. The loudness of the protest suggests that they may in fact think it is. Most likely it's the emotional accompaniment that weighs heavily, rather than the content of the words. However, words are the vehicle by which emotions are delivered and they do have meaning. In focusing on the actual word and its root is unique. With this definition pleasure can be derived from the unwitting and indirect compliment. In this way words can have a powerful positive or negative influence depending upon how they are perceived.meaning a different outcome becomes possible.

Trying to smooth over or deny hurt feelings leaves the impact they have had untouched. To offer reassurance or comfort can help in a limited way, but does nothing to further understanding. However, if one were to ask what stupid meant, it might trigger a look indicating that to ask such a question was pretty stupid. The attitude could very well be that everyone knows it's a disparaging term referring to a severe lack of normal intelligence. The root meaning can offer a new mind expanding piece of information, perhaps causing the person to pause and reflect. Stupid means to be stunned so you can't think clearly. Often that is precisely accurate as to what was felt at the time. A wider picture of what has taken place is thereby presented, softening the assault on one's feelings. Even when a word doesn't exactly fit the experience, the process of searching for meaning points to an alternative solution other than to be hurt, having to withdraw, or retaliate.

It is not uncommon to be called dumb or idiotic, with these disparaging terms eliciting painful feelings. When dumb is defined as an inability to talk, the word may not apply to the surface of what occurred, but it might if there were things left unsaid. An idiot is one who is unique. With this definition pleasure can be derived from the unwitting and indirect compliment. In this way words can have a powerful positive or negative influence depending upon how they are perceived.

Chapter 10

Insanity Can Drive You Crazy

It is not unusual for different words to be used to describe the same phenomena, or for the same word to be used to describe quite different phenomena. If this happens in relation to a complex topic of great importance it can only add to whatever confusion already exists. In this regard the words crazy and insane are a prime example. Although their meaning and significance are world's apart, all too often they are utilized interchangeably as if they were synonyms.

Crazy means in pieces; referring to what may either be a temporary or chronic state of mind. It may involve a transient moment wherein a person is shattered or fragmented by an experience, so that all of their faculties are disconnected and hence not functional. In that sense the person is in pieces or crazy. The person's reactions in such a state may even momentarily be strange or bizarre and their thinking clearly disordered. For others this state of mind may be more permanent. The implication is that in that frame of mind a person's perceptions of reality are completely unreliable at best, and are given absolutely no credibility.

The truth of the matter is that when a person is in pieces (crazy), they may be, and probably are, more tuned in to certain aspects of reality with a laser beam like focus. Even subtle nuances, not noticed by others, are then seen or at least reactively responded to for what they are rather than what they pretend to be. This is not surprising, for the state of craziness itself almost demands a kind of hyper vigilance to what is noxious and what is trustable in the outside world. Consequently the person, out of necessity, sees more deeply and clearly into selective realities

Insanity means that reality is distorted. Therefore it is quite a different matter when a person has had to organize varying aspects of themselves into maintaining a rigidly held view of the world, and in order to insure that nothing will encroach upon that stance reality must be distorted. This frame of mind would not be accurately described as crazy, but as insane.

A crazy person may be quite sane, whereas an insane person may not be at all crazy. In fact the insanity is often created to prevent becoming crazy. Of course it is possible for someone who is crazy to also be insane. Sometimes at first glance the distortions of reality may not be apparent, particularly if the person is especially adept at producing rational explanations. Once a closer look is taken the distortions may very well be noticed, but exposing it to the person even with clear evidence usually does little to change it. Generally the effort to rationalize is only intensified. The word rationalize seems to fit perfectly; divided into two words it becomes "rational-lies".

It is not unusual when insanity dominates in a person's view for there to also be a driven compulsion to enforce that view upon others. With those to whom they are closest the demand may escalate to the point of insisting that it either be accepted, supported, or even adopted. When the person upon whom it is imposed is in a shaky or tenuous position the strength of the demand can "drive them crazy". Making the distinction between crazy and insane can be helpful, at times crucial, in maintaining one's sanity.

The importance of these kinds of considerations was illustrated in the treatment of a 14 year old boy. He was referred due to his parents and school's frustration in knowing how to handle him. He was almost always right and fiercely determined to defend his position. Consequently, he refused to do homework since noone could give him a reason that he considered to be sensible. He could always prove to school authorities that their reasoning was in some way faulty. The authorities would then take an arbitrary stance and he would laughingly mock their attitude. His teachers had become quite upset, but none of the actions they took seemed to affect him. No matter what was tried, he simply smiled or laughed.

Although I had not as yet seen this child, this description was familiar to me. Whether my impression would turn out to apply to him remained to be seen. However, it sounded as though he was very much in tune with the way people in authority will distort reality in subtle ways, making it sound logical, when there is probably a hidden agenda in the positions they take. This child seemed to have a laser beam focus on the underlying truths that were being ignored. Instead of being given credibility, he was seen as seriously disturbed. Although he probably is, in all likelihood he possesses the sanest view point in the area he is seen as having the most trouble. In other words what is labelled as sick is probably healthy, whereas the elements of sickness are either hidden, labelled as healthy, or both. It hints that this child possesses the kind of vision one might have who has in some way been shattered, and hence is crazy. Yet the rigidness of his stance, his arbitrariness and refusal to consider another point of view. suggests some areas at least of insanity as well. When others confronted him with his delusions (distortions of reality) his fight against seeing it appeared quite desperate. My guess at this point was that both factors co-existed.

At home he was in a constant battle with his parents. In their words, he refused to face or accept reality. An interesting comment on their part, for in one sense it probably was true. In another sense it might not be true, in that he might be crying out for his parents to be doing the very thing they were asking him to do. He had many interests and was involved in a host of projects that required alot of concentration and effort. They were limited, however, to activities that he enjoyed, for he totally refused to extend himself if he had no interest. He was creative and effective in what he did, but only on his own terms. When given some other job he would steadfastly refuse. There were also episodes of extreme temper outbursts, particularly with his mother and younger brother. These explosive moments were usually triggered by an injustice, and seemed to have a large element of control. His mother felt very guilty as he was frequently quite accurate in his perceptions.

Here was some validation by a parental figure of this quality in her child. He insisted on the truth in such a way that it was painful for her to truly hear and take in. His father, on the other hand, was a pragmatic person and wasn't at all concerned about the quality of his son's performance. He was worried about his inability to live "within the system". Here was the other side; a parental figure who in a quiet, but forceful, way was attempting to impose a distorted view of reality. He gave "rational-lies", which would be hard to dispute, but it was the kind of insanity that could drive one crazy.

In summary this child was seen as spoiled, lazy, undisciplined, living by the dictates of his grandiosity, and unable to adapt to the "real" world. Earlier there had been several attempts to seek professional help and, though he didn't object or resist going, after one or two sessions he refused to return.

He came to his first appointment willingly, as he had done in the past, and spoke openly of his parents and school's concern. His descriptions were exactly as his parents presented. If he saw a reason for doing something he did it gladly. but noone gave him valid reasons that made sense to him. Furthermore if he voiced disagreements noone showed him where he was wrong. They only insisted he do as others did, or stated that it was in his best interests.

In hearing this I was receiving some limited verification of what I had speculated before I had seen him. He was taking a firm position, indicating an openness to being shown where he was off base, while vehemently refusing to have someone else's viewpoint imposed upon him. On the surface, up to now, there was no sign of his being shattered, and as yet no evidence of his perceptions of reality being distorted.

He spoke of his varied activities and of his friends. Relationships were valued highly and he was deeply concerned with all of the injustices that occurred in the world. In this context he mentioned two people he had found who gave him good reasons for doing things. One was a piano teacher. He played the piano by ear and was pleased by how well he did. Everyone was upset that he refused to read music. They saw his talent and were angry when he did little to develop it. The piano teacher did not try to reach him to read music, instead he tried to help him develop his own skills. He gave him some disciplined exercises to follow, explaining how they could help to bring out his potential. The other was a Hebrew teacher who explained the importance of learning the language. He had begun with no intention of learning, but the teacher talked to him about the language linking him to his forefathers and he applied himself. The teacher also emphasized the importance of being a unique person and he was so impressed he invested himself in studying the new language. After talking non-stop for sometime, he paused to ask me what I thought about the things he said.

I had been listening to him describe what sounded to me like a desperate fight to maintain his autonomy, separateness, and individuality. In doing so I was just starting to become aware of sensing some as yet unseen, underlying vulnerability. This had only been hinted at but largely left unsaid. I was also aware that in talking about his teachers he might indirectly be expressing what he would need from me if we were to establish a working relationship. Taking this into account I told him I thought he had been showing me some of his most valued attributes. I could see how important it was for him to make sure that he wouldn't conform to anyone else's expectations and that he wanted to have the strength to stand up for his beliefs. I also heard how crucial it was for me to give him a reason for us to work together. This made me wonder if his question wasn't coming from his sensing that I thought he had left alot unspoken, which probably had more to say about a reason for him to see me. With these words he interrupted me to ask defiantly, "What do you mean?".

This reaction on his part made me think I had touched a sensitive area within him, perhaps a place where he had been shattered. It could very well be driving him to so vigorously hold on to his unyielding posture. Therefore I said to him that I thought he was fighting hard for his rights, but wasn't very effective at it. I also was sensing there were things he hadn't mentioned that might hamper him alot. Furthermore, what he told me about his teachers spoke to what he needed from me if we were to continue meeting. He then stated, "I want you to listen. There are things I simply can't talk about. I know this is a place to talk, but there are some things I just won't tell you". He was absolutely adamant.

It seemed to me that he was now showing me an area of his insanity, and along with it his fear of having it exposed. He was assuming that I would be harmful or hurtful to him before he had evidence of that being the case. Rather than questioning my trustability, which would be fitting and necessary, he steadfastly was convinced that there was no other possible outcome. By implication he was anticipating a demand for him to conform. At the same time his response indicated that my speculations were quite accurate. I considered his willingness to let me know as a positive sign, and revealed that he was acutely aware of being injured and maybe shattered. I then simply remarked that I thought he was revealing the things he didn't want to speak about out loud all of the time. Therefore he could be wondering if I either didn't notice or whether I wouldn't let him know if and when I heard something. Much later he informed me that it was at this moment that he decided to begin his treatment. It was the first time he felt the possibility of being able to talk.

This child did not feel safe enough to allow his vulnerable experiences to be openly expressed. His fierce fight for separateness and autonomy barely concealed how much he was struggling to keep them hidden. It looked like he expected me to challenge his defiant attitude, or impose a demand upon him. For me to do so would certainly serve to justify his view of the world, but also leave his unspoken appeal for help unheard. My impression was that he was caught in a terrible dilemma; in that the very thing he needed to reach what was torturing him inside he couldn't tolerate. However, he did give some direction as to the conditions he would require in his description of his two admired teachers. This involved supporting his autonomy and striving for mastery, while not being controlled by him. The exact nature of his trouble was as yet unseen.

In the early months he focused upon his wide ranging interests, and a constant theme inadvertently showed itself. It had to do with his worry over danger, injury, and destruction. When it "slipped out" he made a joke over it. For example, in describing his interest in magic he laughingly wondered what someone would do if they were missing a finger, or how a person with no arms would use a computer. During this time he seemed to be working hard to avoid feeling anything with any intensity. Then one day he came in tearfully, signalling me to be quiet. He went on to say that he couldn't talk and wanted me to forget about it. With these words he joked about the impossibility of doing it when someone tells you to. Slowly and hesitantly he revealed a fear that he had never put into words to anyone before. When he went to bed each night he was absolutely terrified. The feeling he had was of someone in the closet ready to come out and attack him. He knew it was ridiculous and made no sense, but he always had to engage in some rituals in order to distract himself. Finding himself so frightened and helpless completely mortified him. The result was in his having a great deal of trouble getting to sleep, which nobody knew. He had kept it hidden feeling it was a sign of weakness. The fact that he was telling it to me now shocked him, yet even in doing so he was left with no idea of what to do about it since telling me made it no better and no worse.

He was finally beginning to bring out in the open some of what he thought he could never express. It did show his underlying fear and how readily it could escalate. I would picture the anxiety reaching panic proportions, ultimately fragmenting his whole sense of himself. It certainly made the rigid positions he took more comprehensible, especially when he could see others gave him no credibility.

He went on to elaborate on his fear. It came out after he had learned about his grandfather's serious illness, which made him frightened over the whole idea of someone dying. This is what he was filled with when he came in. He had wanted me to be silent so he could bring it up in his own way, for he didn't want me to pull it out of him.

This aspect of our relationship was so crucial. He had to be confident that he had the freedom to communicate in whatever way was possible at any given moment. By implication he was accustomed to having others views imposed upon him, and the impact of it "drove him crazy". The following session took place shortly afterward.

I had received an upsetting phone call just prior to our time. When he came in he looked at me and asked, "Do you believe in ESP?" Before I could answer he went on to tell me of his interest in ESP, telekinesis, reincarnation, and other mystical phenomena. He was quite hesitant as he spoke stating that he had to be careful as to who he told about it. "People think you're crazy if you believe in these things unless they believe in it too, otherwise they look at you as strange. If they believe in it, you can share your experience". While he was talking I became aware that the effects of the previous phone call had lingered as he entered the room. It made me think he had perceived my reaction, perhaps unconsciously, and feared it would color the way I looked at him. I then told him I thought he had picked up an upset in me and feared it would influence what I heard from him. He became silent before making a remark about his piano teacher's encouragement of him. After a pause he returned to talking about ESP and all of the things he sensed in other people. He gave numerous examples of how adept he was in picking up on others' hidden unconscious messages, feeling proud of his ability to do so. When what he sensed was friendly, in tune with and accepting of him, he was relieved and comforted. However, when he sensed something disturbing but couldn't tell what it was he became frightened. He stopped, looked up, and asked, "Was there something?, would you tell me?"

He was now openly revealing his sensitivity to others reactions, including my own. More importantly, with some desperation, he was pleading with me to validate his perception.

I said to him that clearly when he first came in I was not ready to listen. He seemed to be checking to see if that had changed and whether I could truly hear him now. His demeanor softened as he spoke of how preoccupied he had been with his fear of what was in his closet. He kept going over it in his mind and suddenly realized that what he feared was inside not outside of him. His sensitivity to feelings in other people, particularly those that were discordant or that he didn't understand, had so frightened him he thought everything he feared was outside of him. That's why he was confused about the closet. He knew noone was there, but the fear was exactly the same as if someone was hiding ready to hearm him and he had sensed it. It felt good to recognize that his feeling about the closet was connected to something hidden within himself.

The gradual development of trust in a relationship, in conjunction with his input having credibility, had allowed this child to gain clarity in distinguishing between what was inside and outside of him. From the position of being shattered he could see reality clearly, albeit in a narrow way. At the same time, however, from the position of having to hold himself together other aspects of reality were distorted. The result was in constantly shifting from craziness to insanity; creating confusion and chaos in himself and others he came in contact with. When he was in transition, tenuously intact, others insanity drove him crazy. He was moving closer towards unearthing the source of what had shattered him, as well as identifying the reasons for his adopting such a rigid protective attitude. In doing so he was experiencing a pulling together of fragmented aspects of himself, as his need for exposing others insanity and sustaining his own diminished.

It surprised him to think about his fears in what was a new way. He could look at his own thoughts just as he had with others, searching for their unconscious meaning. Stopping, he added, "There is something I've never told you. It looks to everyone like I'm very creative and do alot. The truth is I never finish anything". He described coming to the end of a project and abruptly abandoning it. Approaching its completion he felt scared and then either tried to make it look like he had lost interest or had actually finished. "There's something about ending a job that's scary. Oh. When I said that a song went through my head. I'll bet that's a message from inside of me". He paused and remarked that he felt silly even though he knew what was happening was important. "I want to be able to let things come into my mind and think about it". He puzzled about the song and recalled it was titled, "My Life". The song had to do with someone's life ending. It must be telling him that finishing a task was like ending his life. He felt so terrified of his life suddenly stopping that he couldn't complete anything. It was just like something in the closet. He then laughed, commenting on a funny thought. "Something in the closet feels like something in my mind that I've kept closed off. It's trying to come out and give me a message". He smiled broadly, revelling in how good it felt to think this way. Previously he had been afraid, pulled back, avoided thinking, and was left feeling humiliated at being so scared. It felt like something was expanding to allow him to think.

To his surprise he then recalled a story his mother told him that never made sense until this moment. She told him that as an infant he was extremely special to her. However, when he started to assert himself she got so enraged and unable to tolerate it that she ended up beating him. This led her to seek therapy for herself.

Later his brother was born and she repeated the same thing with him. My patient had reacted to the birth and infancy of his brother with intense hostility, which she thought grew out of his having been beatten. What he suddenly understood was whenever he looked at his brother he felt compelled to hit him in a specific manner. He liked his brother so his reaction seemed strange. The way he hit his brother was identical to how his mother had hit him.

The combination of integrating the shattered aspects of himself, along with yielding his rigid defenses, enabled his mind to expand. Memories, thoughts, feelings, and realizations appeared that had been impossible for him to receive before. Initially he had refused to talk. Later this was recognized as a reaction to a deep feeling of humiliation over being unable to adequately describe his trouble. He anticipated and feared that I would expect him to talk about things he could hardly bear to think about. With all of his intellectual capacities, and vast array of skills, he was least capable of dealing with what threatened him the most; that was to be a separate, autonomous human being. In addition, for him to be successful in any undertaking it required that he perceive what was too frightening. In becoming introspective he was finding a new, constructive response to his infantile dilemma. He was facing his deepest anxieties.

Earlier the unknown had been much too frightening to contemplate, and the process of internal exploration could only go so far. Once he touched upon anything unknown he had to turn away and then justify it so as not to feel vulnerable and humiliated. This was the area in which his insanity showed itself. When he felt safe enough his attitude toward the unknown began to change, until it became an opportunity for new learning, rather than a paralyzing terror. It was striking to see how much his sensitivity to the hidden communications of others was echoing with, and became confused with, the way he imagined what was unseen in his closet. With others he could both observe and think about the hidden meaning of what was unseen. It showed how he took in and perceived accurately every nuance of this aspect of external reality. At those moments he was quite sane. If he sensed their reactions were friendly toward him he was reassured, finding pleasure in his discoveries. However, if he couldn't figure them out, or if they were negative and he couldn't find a reason for them they felt ominous.

There is an important lesson to be learned from all of this. Noone is really immune to having pockets or islands of insanity. Certainly any biases we harbor, or judgements we make fall into this category. Exposing them is essential for our own growth and well being, as well as for developing constructive relationships with others. Whenever a person finds themself adamantly insisting on the correctness of a point of view, it deserves being looked into for evidence of insanity. The input of others can then be received as a welcome source of information, not to be blindly accepted, but to be examined for its validity.

Chapter 11

Finding Your Temper

It is very interesting to me how people almost always refer to explosive outbursts of anger as losing one's temper. More often than not it may represent the finding of a temper that had previously been lost. Of course what is generally meant is that a person has lost control of their temper, which is an entirely different matter.

I recall a friend who prided himself on his laid back approach to life, and who rarely, if ever, exhibited any outward display of anger, finding himself erupting in a rage filled reaction to a new puppy's refusal to obey him. He was, at first, quite chagrined and concerned that such a fit of anger could envelop him so completely. Trying to grasp where these strong aggressive feelings came from left him in a quandry. He was acutely aware that the intensity of his reaction in no way fit what set it off, so he knew he had found something that had previously been hidden somewhere inside of him. Clearly he had found his temper, and with it an opportunity to know more about himself.

In a similar fashion a 6 year old boy had come to see me because of his inability to either feel or control his bowel movements. What very quickly emerged was his noticing how this had started with the birth of a younger brother. Once he found his hidden rage at being displaced from the lofty position he had held in the eyes of his parents, he also found the lost connection with his bodily processes.

Both of these situations involved finding feelings that had been made inaccessible. It is not just a semantic matter. When it is defined in this way a pathway towards a new way of looking at it is opened up, fostering the process of becoming a more complete person.

This kind of difficulty was evident in the treatment of an 11 year old boy. He was initially referred because of his mother's concern that the treatment he was currently receiving was not working. She was convinced that he harbored many intense feelings about a divorce occurring when he was age 4, and his treatment seemed too superficial to reach them. The child was also unhappy about his treatment and pleased at the prospect of seeing someone new. The mother also believed that he needed to see a man because this influence had been lacking in his life.

He turned out to be extremely verbal and bright, and most upset by his eye blinking tics and the hurt he experienced in being teased by classmates. He felt very close to his mother, describing her as special. Everything she did was helpful, especially the way she was always there for him and understood his feelings. Right from the outset he wanted to make sure I knew how important she was, in the process showing how protective he was of her. He always tried very hard not to oppose her or go against her wishes.

This child exhibited clearly how much effort he was constantly directing toward creating an impression of himself as kind and considerate. His entire approach to every situation he met was to make sure that he did not either show or even feel anything that could be seen as dissatisfied or complaining much less angry or hostile. It was of great importance that negative feelings could be talked about, but certainly not acted upon. Even the slightest emergence of such feelings had to be quickly moved away from.

In talking about himself he used many psychological terms. For example, he spoke about missing his father in the past but felt he had come to terms with his absence, and then added that there might be some remaining effects in his unconscious. The only thing he was aware of was a resentment of his stepmother's pregnancy. He thought he might be jealous because he was no longer the center of attention during his visits. It reminded him of how often he was called a show off, which hurt his feelings since he didn't think it was true. As far as he was concerned he was just being himself. It was like he would have to hide his talents to keep from being hurt. In this context he wanted me to know of his exceptional ability to be in touch with his unconscious. He had a dream that he thought showed it most clearly. A bad man was shooting bullets at him in a way that could have been frightening. Even in the dream, however, he knew he was dreaming and changed the bullets into candy bars and the man into a favored aunt. This danger thus disappeared.

It was apparent from the outset in his entire demeanor that hostility, anger, and aggression of any kind was very frightening to him. The imagery of the dream vividly portrayed how he handled his anger, so that when it finally reached him it would be hard to recognize it as anger. Candy bars and a favorite aunt were a far cry from a bad man and bullets, yet one was an extension of the other. He had truly lost his temper.

In all likelihood this was involved in his exaggerated need to be so cautious in regard to his feelings about his mother. It was probably in some measure behind his inordinate concern about safeguarding a caring image of her.

During the early sessions he outwardly looked to me as a source of knowledge, inspiration, and guidance. At the same time there was an unspoken attitude implying that he didn't think I knew much at all and that I would undoubtedly ignore the most significant parts of whatever he communicated. He anticipated that I would be pleased by his admiration of me and overlook any hints of negative feeling that may reside inside. There were many indirect references to people who avoided unpleasantness because they were either helpless or unwilling to do anything about it. I commented on how he seemed to need to see me in a positive light, much as he did with his mother, and wondered if he wasn't keeping more disturbing feelings hidden. He vigorously denied that this could in anyway be true, going on to emphasize how he was perfectly capable of recognizing his deepest feelings. Furthermore he could also tell when he was, and was not, being defensive. I simply listened and made no further comment.

He began the next session by reporting a dream. His favorite aunt was walking down a railroad track with a train bearing down on her, perilously close to hitting her. The dream shifted and he was running up to tell his father of the calamity that had almost taken place. His father reacted as though nothing unusual had happened, quietly said hello, and invited him to dinner. In thinking about the dream he realized that when he insisted he held only positive feelings towards me, and I silently accepted it, it meant to him that I only wanted to hear good things. In the back of his mind he knew he was often annoyed and irritable, but was afraid to say so. He wondered why I didn't confront his defensive posture, and help him to talk about the powerful feelings he didn't know how to express. It reminded him of his father who payed little attention to emotional meanings. He wanted to be close to him, but it was too frustrating. After pausing, he noted how fearful he was of asserting himself. It felt like he would lose everything if he did.

He was correct in his assessment of how I had avoided confronting him, and in calling it forcefully to my attention had taken a big step forward in asserting himself. In the face of his emphatic denial I had retreated, readily reminding him of his father. It was a sign of his beginning to find his lost temper, since self assertiveness is fueled by regulated aggression. The dream made the extent of his anger clear to him, captured in

the symbolic image of a powerful train. His annoyance and irritability were further evidence of his anger coming out of hiding.

In the following sessions there was a marked change in his attitude towards me. He had become more spontaneous and aggressive in his approach. Typically he would enter the office bombarding me with questions concerning my personal life, fully expecting that I would refuse to answer. He was prepared to argue with me about it, and was taken aback when I indicated a willingness to respond if it was really important to him. I then added that it might be more useful to discover what was pushing his questions. He teasingly remarked, "Well, that's enough about you", before getting serious and revealing how scared he was of someone dying. The fear was so great he couldn't stand thinking about it so he was always looking for some distraction. Still it was constantly in the background that he could lose his mother and be left all alone.

Certainly the absence of a father both physically and emotionally had contributed to his difficulty, as he only had his mother to hold onto as a reliable figure. When I had tried to call attention to his subtle depreciatory attitude by referring to his fear of being openly critical of me, and then was silent in response to his protest, it unveiled the whole arena of the anger with his father. He quickly saw how hungry he was for me to do what his father could not. That is; help him face these powerful, unmanageable feelings, and express himself assertively. The dream had also reflected how frightened he was that his mother would be as over-whelmed by such feelings as he was. He felt as powerless to save her as his father was. Once he could see this within himself the tenor of his relationship with me changed. He became more assertive and in the process revealed the fear of his mother dying leaving him alone and unprotected. His reasons for "losing" his temper were emerging from out of the shadows.

He then began to feel bored, putting pressure upon me to play games with him, and insisting that we could talk better that way. Whenever I commented on his demands as a way of distracting himself, it only served to intensify them. At the same time he became more irritable and his eye blinking tic more pronounced. I finally commented that I thought he simply did not have words to talk about some of his feelings, yet it looked to me like his body was expressing what he couldn't say. His attitude immediately shifted. At first he was interested in knowing what I meant, but upon discovering I was referring to his eye blinking he became noticeably embarrassed. He then wanted me to tell him what I thought his body was communicating. I said it did bring some things to my mind, which I'd be glad to tell him. However, at this point they would be my stories. Perhaps if I told him what I made of his eye movements it could help touch some things in him; my stories could possibly then lead to his. He got excited about par-ticipating with me in this manner, after noting that the words his story could also mean history. I told him that it made me think he had seen something; either very frightening or overstimulating, perhaps sexual in nature, and had then tried to keep it out of his mind. His eyes could then be expressing a wish to both look and not look, all at the same time.

While I was talking he periodically interrupted to elaborate on whatever I was saying. In the process he developed intricate fan-tasies of sneaking into his mother's bedroom unseen, and going on to imagine observing sexual scenes. He visualized becoming wide-eyed in amazement, wanting to remain a hidden observer. At another point he pictured himself slinking back to his room, feeling cut-off and alone. This made him stop and in a serious vein noted these were all things he was making up. He was certain he couldn't recall any such experience. The only thing it brought to his mind was the early period of his parents' divorce. He remembered feeling frightened about the break-up and sad about the loss of closeness to his father, who moved away to another state. Later he felt terribly uncomfortable in visiting him, as though he was a stranger, until he finally could accept the fact that his father would never know him very well.

Looking back his demands upon me to play with him most likely grew out of the fact that he had no words to communicate the source of his trouble. Thus he felt completely frustrated until I did understand his predicament. My offer to provide the words as a means to gaining access to his deeper feelings had a striking effect. It seemed to make him feel both safe and confident, creating an atmosphere in which he felt protected. This allowed him to playfully fantasize around the theme I provided of coming into contact with his parents sexual activities. Although the impetus was my story, it did prove helpful in freeing up his capacity for fantasy. This led him to recalling his fear and sadness at the time of his parents divorce (his story).

This interchange showed the importance of his separating out what belonged to me, enabling him to see and reveal that his trouble centered upon the dangers of aggression.

In succeeding sessions this was validated further, as fearful memories returned all possessing the theme of violence. He recalled spending a day with an aunt and uncle at age 5, feeling very uneasy because their children were so wild. A teenage cousin got into a battle with his mother and attacked her with a knife. He cowered in a corner, feeling his life was threatened, which reminded him of the loud arguments between his parents. At one point he noticed with great relief that his eye blinking had disappeared. He could use his eyes normally without the constant inner compulsion to blink.

He was actively engaged in unearthing the root of his difficulty in managing anger and hostility, establishing the ground work for it to enter his experience. His lost temper was coming closer and closer to being found.

Once again there was a shift in our relationship, introduced by his expressing some resistance to coming to see me. He felt annoyed about coming, which he didn't understand, but struggled to find words to accurately describe it. It felt like I was just too distant. The room was too dark, the talking too grown up; everything seemed too serious and gloomy. He wanted to relax, play games with me, take a walk, or do things together. What he wanted was real talk, in real language, and be able to play and be a child. He hated the whole idea of me listening to what he had to say and then interpreting its meaning.

I thought his criticism of what I was doing was right on target, and it pleased me a great deal. The elements of truth in what he was saying about how I conducted myself, equally reflected a similar quality in his overly mature attitude. It was a positive development to see him allowing this facade to fall away. By implication he was also appealing for encouragement of his spontaneity, adding to the prospect of finding his lost temper.

I acknowledged the distance between us, as well as the need to communicate in a genuine way. He was openly touched as I spoke. His eyes became tearful and he mumbled what sounded like an expression of gratitude. I went on to say how much it must make him aware of missing a relationship that could bring to life what he valued most in himself. Perhaps he could also see how good it was that he could express his dissatisfaction and anger safely. Certainly it served to solidify our work together. Upon leaving the session that day he reached over to hug me stating, "You've made my day".

This initiated a period of time wherein he directed his full attention to attacking me, followed by forceful demands to buy him toys, take him on trips, and gratify his every wish. On each occasion I would listen, stand firm, and then offer simple comments to clarify what he was feeling or underscore some insight that he would occasionally express. Then one day he came in angrily accusing me of cheating him, which turned out to be my calling our session an hour when in fact it was only 45 minutes. On another occasion he was checking to see if his words could be heard outside of the office, and probing to make sure there were no breaks in confidentiality. After establishing that he could find none, and emphasizing the importance it had for him, he suddenly picked up the phone to call his grandfather. He insisted that I talk with him, becoming furious when I didn't. Instead of talking with his grandfather, or even refusing, I commented upon his testing to make sure the relationship was just between the two of us. He began screaming out that it was his time and he could do with it whatever he wanted. I then strongly affirmed the truth of his statement, which brought forth a big smile. He paused and spoke of how much it meant to realize the significance of his own words; it truly was his time and he was doing what he wanted to do.

This child's anger was unmistakeable and, though at times on the edge of being out of control, enhancing his entire sense of himself. He delighted in having it accessible. Rather than just talking about it, he was allowing himself to experience it. Equally important to him was for it to center around real matters involving the two of us, and he managed to find a way for that to happen. In finding his lost temper he wanted it to fill him completely.

Shortly thereafter he began a session by ordering me to buy him a toy; there was no harm in it and it wouldn't interfere with our talking. On the other hand we could spend the time going to some special place together. He demanded to know why these things were not possible, this time pretending to have a temper tantrum. With a grin he proudly noted how persistent he was in going after what he wanted. It reminded him of how he could always get his mother to give in to him if he worked hard enough, even when it wasn't necessarily good for him. He was surprised to learn how good it felt to demand, push, scream, and holler without feeling guilty or fearful that I'd either push him away or withdraw. In the midst of all of this he noticed how his attitude about being teased in school had changed. He was no longer frightened about people bullying him, for he was more confident and could stand up for himself. his uniqueness was a source of pride. It was like the ground he stood on felt more firm and solid.

Following the return of many traumatic memories, all reflecting the terror he felt about the violence surrounding him, his symptom disappeared. Yet he was averse to coming to his appointments, which brought out his longing for a playful, involved father who could encourage his age appropriate masculinity. In addition he saw how inhibiting it was to be so afraid of his own anger. He then forcefully demanded that his cravings be met, reacting with intense hostility when I didn't comply. Simultaneously he was giving evidence of welcoming the opportunity to vent his anger safely, while implicitly directing me to remain firm. The defenses he had erected, though they offered some protection, prevented him from growing. Side by side, as his need for them diminished, his spontaneity flourished. The groundwork he needed to contine to develop was much more in place. Along with it his lost temper was found and integrated within his personality to fuel his self assertiveness.

It is very hard to appreciate the price that is paid for losing one's temper, until it is found. Because the resulting non-aggressive behavior usually meets with high levels of approval a person may not be at all aware of what is missed. It is quite possible to live well into adulthood believing it is favorable to not be plagued by the impact and effects of angry, aggressive feelings. Whatever dangers are associated with hostile feelings are thus seemingly avoided. The importance of having access to such feelings for a fuller and richer life is then generally not realized.

It is important to not ignore the other meaning of losing one's temper, referring to the problems that arise as a result of not being able to control it. In that case angry feelings are a constant burden, only too ready to erupt, and seldom available to fuel self assertiveness. Temper then is not so much lost as it is over-controlled, and actively defended against due to its intensity. What is lost is the ability to regulate anger, so that with the exception of momentary usually uncontrolled outbursts, it is largely inaccessible. The useful, helpful features of one's temper is what has to be found.

The treatment of a 35 year old man is representative. Initially he sought help because he was distraught over two areas of his life. The first concerned a love relationship in which he was informed that he was too cold, insensitive, and uncaring, and given an ultimatum to seek help or the relationship would end. The other was in reference to his work where he periodically lost control over his anger, making him feel very guilty and worried about its effect upon others. Whenever these angry eruptions occurred he went over them endlessly in his mind, repeating each step until he could assure himself he had done exactly the right thing.

This was a vivid description of the erosive effect of unregulated aggression. He had no apparent alternative when his anger was touched than to try and somehow control it with his intellectual activities.

In the beginning sessions he worked hard to picture himself as totally in control of his emotions and behavior, yet there was an underlying sense of desperateness. When I commented on this unspoken urgency, he related it to his fear that if he didn't do something about his trouble while he was worried, he would probably not follow through. He also felt it would be essential to meet frequently, for he had a tendency to revert back to his usual ways if anything changed.

My impression was of his noticing the tenacity of his defensive reactions, but also some concern that I might not appreciate the extent of his motivation to be free of his limitations.

Once regular appointments were scheduled he began to engage in repetitive, adversarial internal dialogues with me. He took both sides, giving himself interpretations in my name and then arguing about their meaning as I remained silent. Often he started a session with a statement such as, "I was thinking about what you said about my competitiveness". He would then reflect upon the truth of that idea, then quickly refute it, "I'm really a thoughtful and considerate person and not competitive at all". Continuing in this vein, he used historical events to back up his argument. Intense struggles he described with 3 older brothers could easily be seen as competitive, when he was just trying to stand up for his rights and not be dominated.

This patient was displaying how he was involved in an internal battle, designed to prove to me (and to himself) that he was totally free of hostile aggressive feelings, and only had good intentions. Although intellectualizing defenses were predominant, there were already subtle indications of a perception of me as controlling, while critically demanding that he submit to my views. In all likelihood this pointed to the strong need he had for powerful prohibitions to curb his aggression. In spite of experiencing me as an adversary, he also seemed to expect help and protection pointing to a silent background of basic trust.

At one point I reflected upon his concern about being dominated, noting how he was carrying on this one-sided battle with me. I wondered if he had any thoughts as to why it was so important to him. After a silence, and with great difficulty, he tried to put into words a deep inner sensation that was behind all of his thoughts. Slowly he elaborated upon an intense fantasy concerning me. I was a priest, disguised as a psychoanalyst, with the intent of unearthing his darkest sexual secrets and expose them.

The emergence of this fantasy suggested that his preoccupation with the control of his anger, although a problem in its own right, was serving to mask more disturbing feelings carrying homosexual innuendoes. At first it was a poorly defined sensation, which took more form as it moved into the field of his awareness. While he was describing the fantasy it elicited a soft laugh in me, which I thought he may have heard. It took place at the end of a session and nothing was said.

He entered the next session carrying a cup of coffee, and set it on the table remarking that it was for me. He then explained. It was early in the morning and he was concerned for me, imagining that I would appreciate having the coffee. He wanted very much to be thoughtful and considerate. I simply let the coffee stay there, as he became uneasy about my silence. Finally he said that I must be glad and didn't know how to thank him. I said that so far all I could see was that he wanted to put something into me, what that might be was not clear as yet. After a short pause he referred to his fantasy of me being a priest. He had sensed my laugh, which at first had made him feel hurt. Later the feeling changed. His initial thought was of being mocked, but he then realized that I must have been laughing at the absurdity of the idea. Thinking about it this way gave him some perspective, making him aware of how terrified he was of revealing his sexual feelings perhaps even to himself. As he talked his anxiety increased and his words were interspersed with references to my silence.

Although he was validating my impressions as to the significance of his fantasy, he continued to exhibit a great deal of difficulty in expressing his anger. On the surface he seemed to be bringing me a "thoughtful" gift, but his emphasis upon how considerate he was almost shouted out that alot of anger was contained in the act. In addition my silence was clearly disturbing to him, because feelings were pushing forward from deep within him that I thought he was trying to distract himself from. I did not want to participate in that distraction, and I had not yet fully understood my response to his fantasy. Therefore I was waiting until i had more to say about it, since I felt it had a big impact upon him.

He knew he was trying to say something that frightened him, and after hesitating he recalled a dream from the night before in which people accused him of being a woman. "Why don't you talk!", pausing once again he thought of being fat as a child. He felt effeminate and was often teased and ridiculed by others and he wondered if he was a homosexual. "I don't know what to make of all of this, why won't you say something? Your silence is frustrating, isn't there something you can say?" I remarked where I could see how my silence felt like an attack to him, but I wasn't yet clear as to what he needed to hear. He then spoke about his reactions to my silence. Whenever I was quiet he felt a build up of feelings inside and he wanted me to talk because he felt like my words could ease his tension. That was why he liked to think about my laugh, it gave him perspective. Once again he was silent before stating, "I just remembered what I really thought when I brought the coffee. That son of a bitch is going to sleep on me and I better bring him some coffee to wake him up".

His fantasy had triggered a reaction in me that I had not understood. I was trying to find the meaning of my laughter, while he was working hard to strengthen his defensive posture. In the process he was demonstrating what he did when confronted with a lapse in empathy on my part. At first he felt hurt, suggesting there was a beginning awareness of the extent of his emotional attachment to me. However, he quickly recovered and instead of associating to the experience he began to explain it. All of his attention was directed to his conscious mentation, which gave him a sense of perspective and he felt better. If I had given him an effective intervention, it would have furthered his moving deeper into himself on a background of feeling safe and contained. In its place, though he did mention being aware of his sexual anxiety, there was a focus on intellectualizing his reactions. This emphasis upon rational thinking was reenforcing his usual mode of avoiding conflict.

He had expressed an intense, affect laden fantasy, which was a thinly disguised expression of a homosexual attachment. Consciously I laughed at the absurdity, but deeper down I was affected by this powerful stimulus. He took the surface reason for my laugh, explained it in a search for logic and order, and I was briefly tempted to accept this as true. At the same time he was trying to call my attention to the need to look deeper in his act of bringing the coffee. Consciously he was trying to be "kind and considerate", in his characteristic way of protecting himself against expressing any angry feeling. Underneath it all he was reacting to my "sleepiness" (my defensive reaction to his fantasy), which was finally recognized in his angry statement.

I did have a beginning awareness of an empathic lapse, but hadn't seen enough of my motives to be able to talk effectively about it. My silence was disturbing to him and escalated his efforts to get me to participate with him in avoiding the deeper feelings pushing to be heard. A dream wherein he was accused of being a woman, childhood memories of being fat and effeminate, and concerns over homosexuality were all interwoven with the upsurge of these defenses.

Ultimately I was able to locate the source of my laughter and informed him. The result was in his proceeding further and in doing so he found his anger and aggression much more manageable. Along with this development he was also more emotionally involved in all of his relationships.

The journey towards self discovery almost always runs into many obstacles, is certainly arduous, and filled with difficult tasks, but the rewards are many and varied. Noone can know beforehand what will be discovered, or what will be encountered along the way. Losing one's temper, whether it refers to losing contact with angry feelings or to losing control of these feelings so they have become unwelcome, leaves a large gap in a person's life. The process then of finding one's temper, whether it refers to what was lost or gaining regulation of what had to be controlled, will lead into previously unexplored areas. The person has thus received much more than what they bargained for, and conversely what they received was quite a bargain.

Chapter 12

Trust; A mutual recognition of untrustability

In every human relationship if there is something to be learned, each party in an interaction must have a way of making known to the other how they are being received. The reason this is such a critical factor concerns the necessity for trust to exist, for otherwise there will not be enough openness for new or vulnerable feelings and ideas both to emerge and be expressed. The presence of trust is an essential ingredient, since it creates an emotional atmosphere of certainty allowing spontaneity to reign. Only then can new ways of experiencing the world evolve. It is in this way that each person's mind can expand, and once it has grown bigger it can never return to the same size.

This principle flies in the face of old ideas of what constituted neutrality in a treatment relationship. Prohibitions against self disclosure were once taken as a given, though it has long been recognized that these stances were unwittingly taken more in the service of protecting a therapist than in being of benefit to a patient. This kind of posture was always, in some measure, an obstacle to the very things it was designed to encourage. Certainly if self disclosures are used indescriminately they are an interference, but as a means of facilitating meaningful communication letting someone know just how they are experienced is irreplaceable.

In order to be trustable to an other human being one must be capable of seeing that person clearly, unclouded by troubled areas that can create blind spots. This does not mean that at such difficult moments trust is not possible, for that will depend upon how the lack of clarity is managed and understood. Two separate people must inevitably have sectors of experience that lead to differences in their viewpoint, as well as specific areas of conflict that obscure their vision. It is upon this kind of foundation that trust is established. The experience of participating with another who values one's input, and uses it to further a deeper understanding of themself, leading to a constructive change in their behavior, is a key feature. Trust evolves out of this kind of interchange; as both parties have learned something with a mutual recognition of where they are, and are not, trustable to each other.

Lapses in empathy are a necessary part of any meaningful relationship for a host of reasons. These range from simple misunderstandings to more complex emotional reactions. The fact that this element arises is a problem, which sometimes can be quite severe. However, these situations also provide an opportunity with the potential for both parties to learn. This requires a respectful receptivity to each other's input, while seeking to foster and expand clarity.

The following example taken from the treatment of a very primitively organized young child shows how potentially destructive such lapses can be. It also shows how much can be gained when they are identified, acknowledged and given credibility. The therapist's role in taking the major responsibility is essential, roughly equivalent to that of a parent with a child.

A 4 year old boy was referred to me after being diagnosed on several occasions as autistic, brain damaged, and/or retarded. He was a wizened looking child with no identifiable, communicative speech, and only occasional sing-song vocalizations. He wandered unendingly from place to place and submissively complied to any direction. Initially I had planned to see him in a series of evaluative sessions to determine whether treatment was at all feasible, and if not to aid his family in decision making concerning his future. The family had been advised that institutionalization would probably be necessary, the only question being when.

During the first two sessions he just stood silently, or moved awkwardly around the room in no discernible pattern, while gesturing by wiggling his fingers in front of his poorly focused eyes. He paid no attention to me, as I sat quietly trying to draw any possible meaning from his behavior. In the third session I had some sense that his mannerisms and behavior were like an empty outer shell surrounding some internal experiences that he was either unwilling or unable to communicate. I then told him that I used my hands to reach out and touch the outside world. In watching him it looked like he was admonishing his fingers to keep them from being drawn into exploring that world. From all outward appearances he was unaffected by my words, for he continued to wander aimlessly while gesturing to his fingers.

I then noticed I had begun to think about my next appointment, which made me aware that I had disengaged from him. At precisely the point that I started to wonder about it, he turned to me and asked, "Are you listening?" It was stunning to me to hear him utter these words, since they were spoken exactly at the moment when I had stopped listening. Quite surprisingly he had expressed himself verbally, when he had been reported to have no communicative language. I was amazed and curious as to where these words had come from, and how he had developed the capacity to form them. On the basis of these three words I then embarked upon a psychological journey lasting 14 years.

My immediate answer to his question was to tell him that he was right, I had not been listening. I thought I had been affected by his seeming rejection and had responded by turning away. Many years later he spoke of this moment, but only remembered that my voice had made him feel safe. At this point, however, he looked quite somber as he tentatively began to explore my chair with his fingers.

During this initial period it was hard to determine if I was hearing this child at all. He reacted in a way that gave little evidence as to how I was experienced. After I told him of my perception that he wanted to reach out, he appeared to be oblivious to me and my words and I withdrew my attention. This was clearly an empathic failure on my part, but remarkably it prompted his question. The impact of it made me acutely aware both of my lapse and the reason for it. Afterwards I could let him know and thus validate his perception of it. I was beginning to get a picture of how I was receiving him, but turned away when there was no noticeable response. He had then let me in on a little of what he was like by reacting to my withdrawal. Once this mutual recognition had taken place of how untrustable I was at that moment, he became somewhat freer, behaviorally at least. It was possible for him to first explore my chair and then my body. It wasn't until years later when he would fully validate this moment, when he referred to it as one in which he felt safe.

In spite of his initial communicative sentence there was a long period of time during which he was silent; although he did explore other objects in the room and sometimes my body. Periodically he retreated into his mode of gesturing and posturing. A number of months passed, until one day he brought two toy soldiers into his session; one was wounded and bandaged, the other intact and upright. Without words he portrayed their interaction. His play brought to my attention what was happening between us. I spoke to him of the hurt and damage that had been inflicted on the one soldier, and how stiff and ineffective the other soldier was in addressing these wounds. It reminded me of how stiff and ineffective I felt in finding a way to help him. He gave no immediate response, but the next mmorning he awoke very early and spoke his first sentence to his parents. "Take me to Ferapy".

I thought he was showing me in his play with the soldiers how I wasn't reaching him. When I validated this perception I once again became more trustable to him, which was followed by his relinquishing his autistic defense. My impression was that he had made a strong non-verbal statement of how untrustable I was, which made me aware of leaving too heavy a burden upon him. He needed me to bridge the gap, while I was waiting for him. My background feeling of helplessness was pervading the relationship, until he did discover a pathway to connect with me. Once I could see the problem there was hope. My willingness and readiness to give credibility to his input strengthened the foundation of trust being built between us.

The parents called me and an appointment was scheduled. He arrived looking entirely different. His face was worn and haggard, he looked terrified, and he was restless, irritable, and agitated. The only sounds he made were whining and anguished vocalizations. The picture was of a child being viciously bombarded by some internal process and helpless in managing the onslaught. I spoke softly to him of what I sensed was happening, and as I did I could feel my stiffness dissolve. At exactly that moment he approached me, at first stiff and tentative himself, but then gradually molding himself against me. This continued for several sessions.

Slowly he indicated in his behavior, and then with monosyllabic verbalizations, that my voice was too loud, the lights were too bright, or that outside noises were too harsh. Everything seemed to hurt him. I turned out the lights, drew the shades to diminish the noise level, and shifted his body until I could sense he was in a comfortable position. During this time he was sleepless, and in an almost constant state of terror. Many sessions were spent with me holding him in my arms, as I either spoke quietly or was silent. I recalled his play with the soldiers and talked about the impact of outer and inner stimuli, and of his need for buffering and containment. He then began to communicate verbally, initially from the position of being cradled by me but then shifting to his moving around the room.

Here was now more evidence that trust was growing inside of him. With the dissolution of my stiffness I was able to offer him an experience of being held well, which led to the unfolding of a verbally communicative interaction between us. Once this occurred the possibility of my gaining a more accurate picture of what was needed from me was enhanced. Since this child was able to find a means of getting his perceptions across to me, in the beginning with his question and later in his play, it suggested to me that a potential for growth was latently present. Signicantly, the bond of trust developing between us was initiated through his recognition of my untrustability. The bond was made firmer when my eyes were opened by his words, thereby giving credibility to his input. In acknowledging the validity of his perception the recognition became mutual, which led me to discovering the source. The resulting change in my behavior could then serve to cement the bond, and a pathway for managing inevitable lapses was forming.

There is sometimes a tendency for therapists to overlook the crucial element of taking responsibility for their role in an interaction, because the contribution of a patient to any difficulty that arises may seem so unmistakeably apparent. Patients will unquestionably have large areas of blindness, making them untrustworthy. Certainly a therapist's attention will be focused upon identifying what they are and how they operate, leading to pointing them out so the source can be found. When this takes place the bond of trust is clearly strengthened. Often, however, it will not take place in that fashion when the therapist's part goes unnoticed.

Communication between us had shifted into a primarily verbal modality. At times contained, and at times agitated, he spoke of the internal figures that assaulted him. Only occasionally did he speak of a comforting figure. Agitation mounted in describing the attacks, while he was calm and at ease at other moments. He also spoke of mischievous and fun-loving creatures at which point he smiled. This was the first time he had smiled. His speech was quite soft with many words hard for me to understand. The names he gave to the images that populated his mind, however, came out clearly. The descriptions were accentuated by his entire attitude, which captured the effect these objects had upon him. The "make-a-do's" were the most variable. They changed from mischievous, fun-loving, and impish characters to angry, hostile, troublesome figures, to very frightening and provocative beings who escalated in size. They were always accompanied by either overexcitement or irritability. The name shed some light on his life-long episodes of severe constipation. There had been two occasions that required hospitalization when he had not had a bowel movement for weeks. The "big black pops" were dark, partly hidden stick-like figures. They were extremely explosive and frightening. His whole being was immobilized when he felt their presence. Their prohibitive qualities were unmistaeable. "The big pain" was a maternal image who suffered intensely if anything painful was expressed. Matters involving conflict or psychic distress in turn hurt "the big pain". This figure was constantly whining and commiserating. "Paba" was an undernourished, undeveloped, undefined, deprived and helpless infant.

Interspersed with these figures he also introduced a new one' the soldier. This was a recent acquisition and varied from being firm, steadfast, reality bound, and insisting on performance to being soft, tender, understanding, and warmly responsive. In the presence of the soldier there was always an aura of safety.

When this child was verbally uncommunicative it was difficult to determine what was happening inside of him. Much of my understanding depended upon whatever inferences I could make from his behavior. After he reacted to my withdrawal by asking if I was listening, and I could acknowledge the accuracy of his perception, contact was reestablished. Later, in his behavior, he played with two soldiers in a way that suggested it was an exact parallel of how I was experiencing the interaction. I saw him as being wounded and damaged and myself as stiff and ineffective in helping him. Once I realized it and could indicate my openness to being helped by him, it had a profound effect. His autistic defenses appeared to fall away and a host of stimuli that he seemed oblivious to before were experienced as painful. He was obviously seeking comfort in molding himself to my body, and as my stiffness dissolved I was able to buffer him from the traumatic impact of internal and external stimuli.

The difference between the way in which internal and external stimuli were experienced was reflected in the "make-a-do's" and the "big black pops". The "make-a-do"s" possessed fluctuating instinctual qualities, indicating that they were the consequence of contact with the demands of bio-physiology. The "big black pops", by contrast, were prohibitive in nature, giving expression to this kind of contact with the outer world. Therefore the impinging aspects of the "make-a-do's" were overstimulating, while those of the "big black pops" were attacking (patterned after experience with an explosive father).

His new found ability to communicate verbally furthered my understanding of the powerful forces attacking him from within. The combination of these internal and external stimuli had in turn affected how his self was represented, best portrayed by "Paba", a split-off, damaged, and shapeless infant.

After a time the way in which he wanted to be held began to change. He was quiet while molding himself to my body, but with little animation, irritability, or expressions of any intensity. A pattern evolved of his entering the room and passively making physical contact with me. Although I was concerned about its meaning I said very little until he again brought in the injured and erect soldiers. This time his play was listless, and he dealt with the two as though they were interchangeable. Watching him I was reminded of what was not happening between us. I told him I could see how important it was for him to be held and comforted, but it looked like he was turning away from talking about his inner experiences. I wondered if he wasn't showing me that it was time for me to be like the soldier who knew when to be firm. Maybe the injured soldier needed to use his strengths and not be protected in the old way. At first he had no visible reaction to my words, or to the change in my attitude. He just remained listlessly on my lap. Suddenly, however, he got up, walked to the other side of the room and spoke directly to me. In reference to an upcoming interruption created by my vacation he asked, "Doctor go away?"

I thought the uncertain questioning tone in his voice was expressing his anxiety concerning what he had just experienced in my emotional attitude towards him. Earlier he had sought (and found) comfort in molding himself to my body. However, my impression was that he continued to hold onto this mode of interacting when it was no longer necessary. Whether I was right or not, I did sense a message from him silently expressing a need for me to be more active in encouraging him to utilize whatever resources he had to move forward. Witnessing this shift in his behavior had made me unwilling to comfort him at the expense of his growth. I just didn't want him to be helpless and undifferentiated. Perhaps more importantly, I was starting to believe that he was capable of doing more. I also thought his question displayed his sensitivity to this implied message from me, which then reminded him of my upcoming vacation.

I was gone for several weeks and when I returned he was visibly excited upon seeing me. He proceeded to release an accumulation of feces he had retained during my absence. My immediate response was one of warmth, concern, and affection. I felt a wish to clean him much in the manner of a young infant, and to reestablish the connection interfered with by my vacation. Instead of acting upon what I felt, I held back thinking it was inappropriate to do so. In its place I talked of the anger he must be expressing at having been abandoned. He reacted by becoming extremely withdrawn and reverting to his previous mode of posturing and gesturing. He became almost totally uncommunicative. I knew something had gone wrong, as his behavior made it abundantly clear that I had seriously misunderstood him.

Apparently my departure had involved the return of his earlier attachment to bodily processes. The trusting relationship that we were forming was too tenuous and unstable to be maintained without the reenforcement of ongoing contact. However, it was strong enough that if the conditions were proper it could be readily activated. Upon my return he anticipated finding the support that had been missing, and he immediately let go of the tie to his bowel movements. He was ready to make use of our relationship, which he had been holding in abeyance. Unfortunately my defensiveness created a lapse that awakened and recreated the traumatic experiences so prevalent during his earliest years. The effect was to disrupt the trust that had been developing and to thrust him back into the protective armor of an autistic withdrawal. After considerable self exploration I was able to uncover the source of my inhibition in a personal conflict over my feminine identification. It had arisen in my initial feeling of warmth and affection, blocking me from openly expressing this understanding of his internal state.

Once I informed him of what I was realizing, and how it led to my letting him down, he was able to describe what the experience was like for him. During my absence he had reverted to holding back his bowel movements, terrified that if he let them go he would have nothing left. The moment he saw me he just let loose. Instead of being welcomed, however, the words I used hurt him so he pulled away. Slowly his ability to communicate his thoughts and feelings verbally returned.

For the first time he began to test the limits of our relationship. He was also testing the depth of my understanding of the previous rupture. He did this by searching for objects in the room with the intent of destroying them. With great trepidation he approached a target of his attack, and as his confidence grew he became quite forceful in his effort. On the surface it would have been easy to interpret his behavior as hostile. More importantly I felt he was probing to see if I would recognize that he was really seeking a loving and containing maternal response. It looked to me like he was recreating another version of the situation between us where I had failed him. My initial response was to simply state that I didn't want either he or the objects in the room to be hurt. Anxiously, he went ahead anyway, while I held him gently in order to restrain him. I experienced these interactions as a means of solidifying a bond of closeness, as though I were conforting a very young child who was exploring his capacity to affect the outer world. This behavior was interspersed with, and gradually replaced by, his being able to talk about events in his life. He had never done this before. It was striking to observe how his mind was growing.

He described his interactions with his mother, father, brother, and other children. They all reflected a common theme of his doing all he could to gain some measure of mastery of his environment. He spoke of his fears and frustration, but especially of his anger. Whenever he felt his anger mounting he became noticeably fearful. In the midst of this he developed a fantasy that he and I were special agents, possessing unusual skills and abilities so that we could manage any circumstance. His job was to secure knowledge about others, but there would always be some obstacle that prevented him getting to it. Others viewed him as an enemy who must be thwarted, or from whom any information must be hidden. He would then come to consult with me, for I was the head of all special agents. The two of us would then work together to figure out the problem and in doing so find a way to overcome it. He was delighted with the fantasy and particularly pleased when I would say, "Well, that's a tough one. Let's think about it, see what we know, and find out what can be done". He, in turn, would present to me all of the facts he had available, and we would search for a solution.

The following session was representative and took place just after he learned he would be away for a week, since he was going to attend a family reunion in a distant city. He began by telling me about the trip. He was going on an airplane and scared that the plane would either not get off the ground or crash. Very anxiously he repeated questions to me as to whether that could really happen. "Can the plane crash?, will the plane really fly?" I told him I thought he might be so frightened because in being away from me he was concerned that he couldn't keep an image of me inside. His face lit up as he had the idea that as special agent x-9 he could enter the plane, explore it, and see if it was safe. He could discover its secrets and if there was any sign of trouble he would report it to the pilot. If the pilot didn't listen, or didn't appreciate what he was saying he would know not to fly on that airplane. After a pause he got worried about the return flight. Although he might trust the pilot who brought him there, if he couldn't trust the pilot bringing him back he's be alone in a faraway place. I said it sounded like he was reminding me of the time when there had been an interruption between us and it had ended up in a crash upon my return. I had not been the trustworthy pilot he had known when I left. Perhaps he was concerned that it would be repeated. He was silent for a moment before talking about the reunion, especially how he looked forward to seeing his grandfather. The session ended and that evening I received a telephone call from the airport. He stated, "This is special agent x-9. The airplane is o.k.".

My failure had repeated the traumatic conditions of his early years, and had given me a grasp of his unique sensitivities and of what had gone wrong in his early development. After acknowledging my part in it and reconstructing his infantile traumas he could express what it was like for him. In the process of this mutual recognition of my failure, using his perception of it to bring enlightenment to me, the bond of trust between us was strengthened. He could then continue his movement forward. In addition it allowed me to see things affecting him that he was blinded to, adding clarity to our relationship. At this point inevitable failures could occur and not be so disruptive. The deepening understanding we were both gaining of the impact of lapses in empathy made it possible. In correcting my mistake a greater degree of confidence was growing that meaningful answers could be found, placing our interaction on firmer ground. This element of increased safety allowed him to engage in a physical attack upon my person and belongings. To me it was reminiscent of his initial behavior of admonishing his hands against reaching out. A situation was created in which he could be readily seen as hostile, when he was searching for comfort. Earlier I had imposed my conflict upon him, and it had been devastating. Unwittingly I had become a representative of a hostile world, insensitive to his needs, and to which he could only adapt by retreating into an autistic position. My awareness of the source of the problem encouraged him to test my ability to see clearly enough to help him. Words were simply not enough and so he had to elicit the more powerful impact of a physical interaction. In doing so he experienced his ability to be effective in reaching out to touch the world. He became more visibly introspective, in some ways mirroring my attempts to understand his thoughts and feelings. However, he discovered that in adopting a self observing stance he was able to gain mastery of his anxiety and was more able to deal with the demands of the outer world.

There was a subtle, yet observable, sense of greater stability reflected in his posture and bodily movements. His style of thinking was also different. The internal objects populating his mind, instead of being presences that dominated and attacked him, became mental productions used to express what he was feeling. He could now talk about them as memories, or as facets of his imagination, which was in contrast to his being overwhelmed by the effect they had. He was able to describe a variety of interactions with other people in a narrative fashion, a new development for him. However, when confronted with a physical separation from his treatment, a high level of anxiety resurfaced. He was afraid that the integrative experiences that had come to mean so much to him would be disrupted if he wasn't in actual contact with me. This was expressed in his concern about the airplane crashing or not getting off of the ground. His anxiety also reawakened the traumatic episode that had followed the previous separation. My reading of these concerns seemed to be very helpful, for it indicated my eyes were now opened. An area of untrustability in me had been unearthed, and brought out into the open where it could be mutually recognized and corrected. The end result was in a stronger sense of trust.

After he returned from his trip he was excited and wanted to talk about it, revealing how proud he felt that he had managed it so well. He also noticed how angry he became often with the slightest provocation. At the same time he was terribly frightened of expressing it. In the ensuing months, at first gradually and then with increasing regularity, he became absorbed with this theme. Each session began with a reference to his fear of asserting himself. As he spoke his anger would mount, his body movements become stiff and rigid, and a frightened look appear in his eyes. In vivid terms he emphasized how much he wanted to be angry without holding back, for he felt it was too much to contain. He described situations in which he felt controlled, put down, and forced into submission, which enraged him. It stirred up fantasies of extreme violence.

His attention turned to his admiration of General Patton. He was a hero that he thought was great and he often wished he could be just like him. I reflected on his desire to find these qualities in me so he could make them a part of himself. Upon hearing these words he immediately announced that he had made a decision. He was not going to be submissive, and was determined to no longer hold back his anger. Following this assertion he developed an explosive diahrea that lasted for several weeks, severe enough to cause concern over dehydration. During this time he had the idea that his body was speaking for him, since he could feel how as soon as he decided to vent his aggression he was flooded with more than he could handle. The diahrea finally subsided, and as it did, he laughingly remarked that he had a picture of himself spilling out his anger through his bowels. To his surprise he found himself more able to contain and speak of his rage. However, as he did so he paced back and forth shaking his head and his hands. His entire being vibrated. These mannerisms were somewhat similar to the behavior he showed in the beginning. Now the movements seemed to help him be able to verbalize his feeling. He commented that he felt like a bomb about to explode. Soon he was directing his fury at his mother, as he erupted whenever she made any demand. Her response was to be repulsed, accompanied by a whining appeal, "Why do you have to be this way?" This made him be overcome by a feeling of how bad he was. He found it impossible to be openly angry with his father, because he was so frightened and paralyzed. He kept trying to stand up for himself and express his anger, but when he did it came out with such force that others looked at him as though he was "crazy".

With me any word that I uttered elicited from him a very angrily shouted, "why?" , which was followed by a profound sense of having done something awful. I occasionally commented about his concern that I would be injured by his attacks, or that his anger would provoke me into retaliating. His reaction to anything I said, even before I could get a sentence out, was a furious yell, "Why did you say that"? I would then simply reflect back why I had said it and he would become calm as he murmured, "Oh, I see". He went on to say that he was practicing being angry with me, so he could be more at ease with it. It seemed safe and he didn't feel either humiliated or that he was "crazy". He could just explode without feeling bad. Slowly he did become more comfortable when he was mad and even noticed the pleasure he felt when he was assertive.

Once he felt able to assert himself his thoughts turned to his interest in his genital sensations. He referred to his masturbatory activities and wanted to rub his genitals in the sessions. I was uncomfortable at the prospect of his putting this wish into action, leading me to state that I saw it as his wanting to talk about his sexual fantasies (secretly hoping this would happen). In the following session he entered quietly with a determined look on his face. Finally he shook his head affirmatively, took out his penis and began to masturbate. I said that he must have taken my words as an invitation. He responded by describing the pleasure he felt, adding that it looked to him as if I was the one that was uneasy over what he was doing. This assertive statement on his part made me acutely aware of how correct he was, but also of how much he had changed. I told him how accurate he was, which delighted him as he continued. He recalled how worried he had been whenever his penis got erect, thinking it would break or that there was something wrong with him. I said that my uneasiness must have concerned him and made him think of these fears.

He was silent before recalling a dream from the previous night. He and a man were construction workers building a very high, strong, concrete building. It was unfinished and they were working on the 13th floor. Looking down he could see the remnants of an old rundown shack, which had been removed to construct the new building. He looked up to see how high the building was, but could not see the top.

His whole style and manner of communicating had changed. Now he expressed himself directly with the intent of getting the meaning of his experiences across to me. He was aware of the many defenses he had constructed to prevent his acting assertively. Furthermore he could use my comments to either reject or accept, and those that were consonant with his feelings helped him to bring them out in the open. When he finally decided to vent his hostility it precipitated a body response of severe diahrea. He did gradually achieve more perspective on, and integration of, his aggression, best shown in his laughter at the idea of his rage spilling out in his diahrea. The way he dealt with my discomfort was quite striking, emphasizing how much more solid his sense of trust had become. The confidence with which he asserted himself stood out, for such moments of my blindness were now readily and mutually recognizable. His reporting of the dream, the first he had mentioned, tended to underscore how much his trust had grown. The dream itself reflected the status of his treatment, the growth that had taken place, and the work remaining to be done. The old rundown shack was reminiscent of the shattered and fragmented state of his internal world when we began. The new building, which had reached the 13th floor (as he was in his 13th year), gave a picture of our work. The image of a tall, new building also seemed to represent the sense of intactness of his erect penis and of his possessing enough stability to welcome these sensations. His search for the top of the building might have been the first time that he could consider a time when our work would come to an end. The dream also indicated that this was not yet in sight.

The solidification of trust, along with his ongoing growth and development changed the whole tenor of our relationship. What was now required of me was in the realm of enlarging his self knowledge and awareness. The relationship itself was still an important factor, but not to the extent it had been.

This was shown as his masturbatory actions abated and his concerns were increasingly verbalized. He had seen his mother undressing and was startled to discover she had no penis. Many sessions were spent with him asking questions, repetitively expressing his fantasies, fears, and curiosity. He thought everyone had a penis and couldn't imagine anyone not having one. A flurry of fantasies concerning the reproductive process emerged, interspersed with fragments of information that he had learned in school. He thought babies grew inside of a penis and were born that way. The role of sexual intercourse was familiar to him, but he repeatedly tried to reconcile this information with the trouble he had in conceptualizing the idea of a penis entering the inside of a woman. He could easily imagine a penis entering a man, either anally or orally, which made him giggle. Thinking about genital union with a woman aroused high levels of anxiety, usually reflected in his rigid, stereotyped repetitions of the idea. He seemed to be trying to master the terror with his thought processes. At the same time he was showing interest in the girls he knew in school, describing how exciting and mysterious they appeared to him. When it came to the prospect of initiating any involvement with them, it made him feel totally lost in knowing what to do.

The trust that had formed both within him and in the bond between us was apparent in the following session. I had been a few minutes late in starting, which made him increasingly upset as he noticed the time passing. While waiting he fantasied me being with my wife, but he became more uneasy as he looked at the closed door. With each passing second his fear mounted. I commented on how threatened he seemed to be at the thought of a woman taking me away from him. This led him to talk about different girls he was interested in. He just didn't know what to say to them, and often felt paralyzed. Noticing the strength of his desire made him want desperately to reach out to them. I told him I was reminded of "Paba", the helpless infant, who needed a mother most of all. The mothering he had received crippled him. He fell silent for a long time before his face suddenly lit up. He described a trip he had taken to explore a cave. Some of the rooms were large and some were small and narrow. The largest room was lit so the whole cave could be seen. A guide had turned off the lights to show what total darkness was like. He had felt a sense of dread and impending danger. The guide then turned on a flashlight to point out the openings that went deeper into the earth. He was relieved, for it seemed safe to explore the cave as long as the guide was present to shine a light. This made him realize he was only frightened if he was left alone in the dark.

The difference in what he needed from me was apparent in this association to the cave. He could look into the darkness with the help of the guide's flashlight (my interpretations illuminating the unknown). With the easing of his anxiety he could include within his experience what had been an overwhelming threat.

The meaning of trust and the concept of "good-enough" are intimately interrelated. "Good enough" is frequently misunderstood to signify that noone is perfect. In other words to imply that in spite of one's best efforts there will always be moments of failure, or of an inability to accomplish a goal, or to function as one might like in important relationships. When it is considered in this fashion it would suggest that the task is to overcome whatever deficiencies are present so as to ultimately achieve the goal. In fact, "good enough" refers to the impossibility of two separate individuals to not have moments of a "lack of fit". Furthermore it is precisely in these moments of a "lack of fit" that true learning occurs. Thus being "good enough" is a desirable state in itself. It has to be taken in the context of there being enough of a fit for trust to be present otherwise nothing constructive can take place. In any relationship there will always be places each party is untrustable to the other. The only way that could not exist is for each to be an extension of the other, which is far from a healthy state of affairs.

It is for this reason that for one person to sacrifice themselves, supposedly for the benefit of another, is bad for both parties. The person who sacrifices ends up doing things out of obligation, not being true to themselves or genuine with the other. That person can then only suffer the resulting resentment, usually silently, or be incomplete in how they participate. The other in receiving what is sacrificed may be momentarily appeased, but in the long run robbed of an opportunity to learn. It may be from their hurt, disappointment, or anger, or from the discovery of unrecognized resources within themselves.

It is not unusual for such sacrifices to be thought of as highly desirable. Unfortunately this approach is often highly approved of and even encouraged, with no recognition of its subtly destructive qualities. This kind of behavior may be considered to be quite appropriate, and not even noticed until some event interferes with or disrupts this characteristic way of interacting. Only then will it become apparent that sacrificing serves to shore up a fragile sense of self, or has been designed to regulate self esteem.

This was the case with a college professor in her late 30's who came to see me because of her distress after discovering her husband was involved in an affair with one of her students. Although she had been deeply hurt and felt betrayed, she was most fearful of acting precipitously. She loved her husband and was concerned that in a fit of rage she would end the relationship, when it might be possible to understand the meaning of the experience and feel more receptive to at least consider going on. It seemed to her that there was more intensity to her feelings than could be explained by the circumstance itself. She wanted to gain a fuller understanding of herself, her husband, and of what had happened before making a decision that she might later regret.

In the early sessions she went to great lengths to find exactly the right words to adequately express the nature of the anguish and pain she felt. She was acutely aware of how furious she was and there was some relief in expressing it. The fact that she had been deceived was bad enough, but the worst part was the loss of what she had assumed was an almost idyllic relationship. The affair made her realize just how much effort she had put into building up an image of her husband, and of their marriage, that depended on her directing him on how to behave so as to fit this picture. His infidelity had shattered the image so completely that she saw no way to build it up again. In this regard she felt terribly sad and very uneasy as to how it would affect her life and the lives of her two young sons. She burst into tears as she imagined what it was like for her children.

In mentioning her children, almost as an afterthought, she brought out the many phobic avoidances that controlled her life. They always involved situations in which a child could conceivably be injured, left in an unmanageable predicament, or be faced with an intolerable separation because of some act of negligence on her part. It had expanded to include the harm that could come to a growing fetus if she were to unknowingly become pregnant and then expose herself to something that had even the most remote potential of being toxic. Thus she was panic stricken lest she leave the house without making sure her children were prepared for any conceivable circumstance that might arise. If by chance they forgot a book she would have to bring it to them, for she couldn't stand the idea of leaving them in such a spot. She couldn't pass a microwave oven unless she had her period, because of her fear that some damage would result if she happened to be pregnant. The same applied to whatever she ate or drank, depending on the time of the month. Her life had been scheduled so these situations could be avoided, which was quite a task in managing a career and a family.

She wanted to be sure that I understood the matter of greatest concern to her, since she knew it would be easy to think it was the hurt, betrayal, and rage at having her trust violated. Although these were all true, they were not what really worried her. In the

process she described how much her life was based upon sacrificing herself for others, particularly her children. The extent to
which she "protected" them from the slightest possibility of experiencing pain, discomfort, frustration, or disappointment was
striking. The idea that a child could learn from these experiences
seemed foreign to her. Yet she herself knew how vital it was to
understand what was happening, for the only real protection an
individual can gain is from knowledge. She also made it clear how
essential it had been to maintain an image of a deeply caring
father and husband, who protected his family and was admired
for his sensitivity and warmth. It was this internal picture that had
been disrupted by her husband's affair. She had in no way connected this concern with her phobic symptoms, or for that matter
seen her panic as anything but appropriate. Her acceptance of the
avoidances was remarkable, especially since they interfered to
such a large extent with how she conducted her life. The phobias
theme was significant, in that they involved preventing a child
(born or unborn) from suffering. The implication was that she
would be responsible for creating an irreparable trauma. In addition they focused on things that could actually occur, allowing her
to explain her behavior as an expression of highly valued maternal
functions, thereby enhancing her self esteem. However, she could-
n't help but notice they were designed to alleviate her panic and
resulted in serious limitations in her ability to move freely. All of
this suggested that her attitude toward self sacrifice grew out of
experiences she had endured as a child.

She took some comfort from the fact that she had reacted to her
husband's deceptions right from the beginning of the affair. It
pleased her to discover how sensitive she was to his dishonesty. At
the time she had rationalized her discomfort and suspiciousness
by attributing it to her jealous nature and an overactive imagination. This led her to stress the importance of honesty and trust,

referring to the atmosphere in which she had been brought up. She was the oldest of 4 children, having a sister and brother two and three years her junior and another sister 15 years younger. The emotional climate of her family was extremely confusing during her formative years. Emphasis was placed upon being truthful, while subtle deceptions ruled the day. The children and their needs were considered to be an absolute priority, and indeed every material need and educational advantage was provided for the asking. Any expression of pain or frustration was always met with an attempt to ease it regardless of the cost. The idea of coping with discomfort and learning from it didn't exist. If anything frustrating arose the answer was to ignore it and then find or be given something gratifying to take its place. The expressed attitude was that a child must be shielded from the painful realities of life at all costs. This included hiding the truth of anything that might be disappointing or hurtful, even telling lies if they were thought to be reassuring. If the parents were going out for an evening they would wait until the children were occupied in play and then quietly sneak off "to spare them" the pain of saying goodbye. Similarly if one child received a gift or treat it had to be hidden from the others, so as not to make them feel envious. If it was discovered, something equivalent had to be given. Disagreements or fights between the parents were covered up as if they hadn't happened and if asked it would be denied.

Her mother had devoted her entire life to taking care of her children, longing to be idealized by them, much as she had done with her mother. She was a very dependent woman whose interests centered exclusively on what she saw as her duty in caring for the household. Family loyalties were of primary concern and the outside world was portrayed as a dangerous place. Any evidence of a child striving for independence was met with an anxious, overprotective response. The father, by contrast, was outwardly fiercely independent. He always insisted on doing things his way, and was largely unavailable to his family due to his absorption with work. My patient found interactions with him hopelessly frustrating, since he always had to be right and used quotations from supposed authorities to prove his point. She finally had little to do with him as she got older, and basically thought he played an insignificant part in her life.

It was a surprise to her to find out how eager and excited she felt in coming to her appointments, for she had expected it to be difficult. Instead it seemed like her entire life had become centered around her sessions. She also noticed how impatient and irritable she got whenever I said anything. Even my slightest remark or question felt to her like I was challenging the validity of her words, and she had to fight for their accuracy. It was unmistakeable to her how these feelings were similar to what she had experienced with her father.

In thinking about her excitement in seeing me, she remembered getting up early in the morning supposedly to do her homework. This was the excuse she used to be with her father as he got ready for work. She then was embarrassed as she also recalled taking showers with him and the sexual innuendoes caught her attention. Watching him made her very curious about his body and aroused what she described as a peculiar sense of excitement. These memories made her realize how much she had forgotten about her emotional involvement with him. She had been furious with him when he was away from home, and had wondered just what he did. She also became aware of a host of other questions that had gone unasked concerning her parents sexual relationship. Simultaneously she noticed the same unspoken curiosity about me that preoccupied her when she was away from the sessions. She anticipated that I would consider her questions to be inappropriate, which echoed with her parents remarks that her eyes and ears were too big.

In this regard she was able to put into words how alert she was to my every expression; both looking for and expecting some sign of a male dominant attitude. It was as though she was preparing herself to find and attack it. The emergence of these feelings made it clear to her that she had worked very hard to keep her father at a distance, yet had strongly admired and envied his forceful traits.

The difficulty she had experienced in establishing her separateness was vividly portrayed. Any progressive thrust toward independence was actively undermined by her mother's infantilizing behavior. Real protection was thus quite limited. Her father, while presenting an admirable, independent figure, was incapable of supporting any movement in this direction. He was much too unavailable and her feelings about him much too conflicted and frustrating.

Her thoughts then turned to the significance of her relationship with her mother. She was fearful of getting caught up in, and enveloped by, her mother's encouragement of dependency. She could feel how easy it would be to retreat from any anxiety-laden separation. During her childhood years she escaped by forming an intense attachment to a friend, who was seemingly fearless in moving out into the world. She clung to this relationship for support of her own desire to do so. The friend moved away at the onset of her adolescence, which she experienced as a devastating loss. From that point on she was unable to feel comfortable or be herself with others. She managed it by directing all of her energy into conforming to whatever others expected. She then went off to college, excited at the prospect of being free of her parents' influence, where she met and married the only man she ever felt at ease with.

Initially she saw him as the complete opposite of her father; compliant, flexible, and to all appearances deeply interested in her. She proceeded to finish her schooling, obtain an academic position, and have two children. She was living a fantasy of having an ideal family, a working mother and involved father, proving to herself that it could be done. In the background, she knew she was in the constant position of orchestrating her husband's conduct. It was especially in relation to the children that she had to work hardest to make his image fit. Although she hadn't thought about it in this way, she had not realized how controlling she had been. She knew her husband's mother was very controlling, and could see how she had unwittingly recreated this attachment. It dawned upon her that this was her contribution to his sexual acting out.

This insight was helpful to her, but didn't change the most painful part concerning the lies he used to coverup the affair. It reminded her of her father, best captured in his answer to her question as to whether he had ever been unfaithful. His reply, "Not that I know of" was both ambiguous and deceitful. There was also a shift in her feeling about me, in that she had anticipated I would either avoid her questions or give her vague, non-committal answers. In seeing the link to her father, she now looked to me as someone who would be forthright, genuine, and honest. She could tell that the value she placed on honesty was so extreme, because of the nature of her tie to her mother. Her mother talked about the truth as essential, but was deceitful and justified it as necessary to prevent hurting others. It was obvious that it only protected her. She saw her mother as totally incapable of saying no, always sacrificing herself to meet any expressed wish. This made it vital for my patient to have firm, dependable limits to help her feel safe.

Shortly after this discussion she requested a change in her appointment time. I thought, and told her, it sounded like a need for me to remain firm. In back of my mind I knew it would be an inconvenient time to arrange. That night she had a dream in which she was talking to me and noticed I had a very peculiar hairdo. In thinking about the dream, the hairdo was an exact replica of her mother's. I said I thought this part of the dream reflected her perception of the inaccuracy of my comment about the change in time. I was using her yearning for firmness to cover over my need for the appointment not to be changed. Her face immediately lit up, for she had observed my words didn't feel right to her. She could sense there was something else behind what I said. Bringing it out in the open felt good, and in contrast to what she felt as a child. Whenever she sensed her mother was hiding something from her, in her imagination it was something awful and she couldn't bring herself to ask. She didn't have words before, but now could see it was how unreliable her mother was. She gave the impression that her child's needs were a priority, yet she knew she would be suddenly dropped if her mother was threatened in any way. The sensation was identical to the panic she experienced when she was separated from her loved ones in unfamiliar surroundings. She imagined a catastrophe like an earthquake keeping her apart from those close to her. It was also the fear she had if I failed to understand something.

This insight was liberating to her. She was able to identify how she had become so overinvolved with her children, constantly sacrificing herself to make sure their every need was met. Often she knew it was in their best interests to say no, but found herself unable to do so. She expressed admiration for my search for the truth, applied it herself in dealing with her children, and it was quite helpful. Each time she was forthright in her dealings with others she felt stronger. Along with it she was able to help herself and her children move into the world with a sense of adventure and excitement. Her phobic attitude toward separations gradually faded and dissolved.

At this point she had a dream in which she was with me observing how I cared for a baby. She was watching my behavior and comparing it to what she would do, taking note of the similarities and differences. She could see clearly what was best for the baby and corrected me when she thought I was wrong. This dream felt like a turning point for her, as it reflected her ability to utilize the therapy and at the same time have confidence in herself. This turned out to be a significant moment, since vivid fantasies began to emerge. At first they centered around a powerful wish to become pregnant, accompanied by a desire to proudly exhibit it especially to women colleagues. The fantasy gave her a feeling of elation, like she had won a victory. However, there was a worry that if she let it be known she would be faced with some tragic consequences. The uneasiness was relieved when she recognized the rivalry it expressed with her mother, followed by an opening up of her sexual feelings. Previously she was so controlled in sexual situations that only the dimmest sense of being aroused was present. She had associated sexual arousal with losing control and thus had to occupy her thoughts with other matters to prevent a sexual response. She now was welcoming her fantasies, for in discovering their source she was finding a whole new perspective on her childhood, as well as her current life. She had come to see the price she had paid for sacrificing herself on the one side, and the debilitating effect it had on those close to her on the other.

All learning involves trial and error, so that making mistakes is a crucial element in being able to grow. However, if those mistakes are held onto, and misidentified as a valuable means of conduct-ing one's life, the degree of trust that can be allowed in a relation-ship becomes very narrow. There is then little room for spontaneity or for widening one's horizons.

Chapter 13

Don't Forget to Play

After I had completed the adult portion of my psychiatric training, I was moving into my major interest of working with children. I became very concerned because I was not understanding the children I was seeing. It surprised me, for I had always connected well with children in a variety of roles and situations. I enjoyed playing with the children of family and friends, as well as teaching them as a camp counsellor and swimming instructor. This was the first time that I had contact with children where I did not feel comfortable. and where i did not feel particularly sensitive to what they might be feeling. My teachers and supervisors in the training program seemed quite pleased with what they thought of as my progress, but I knew something was wrong. Finally I approached a woman who did nothing but work with very disturbed children and who had an aura of wisdom about her.

She listened carefully as I explained as well as i could just what worried me, and after a time simply asked when I was going to enter the room. Here I had been describing to her in great detail how I had been interacting with the children, so it took me awhile to grasp what she meant. I then realized she was refering to the seriousness of my attitude, and her question was pointing out to me that I was keeping a significant part of who I was out of the picture. In her view, she couldn't imagine how I could understand anyone from such a distant position and certainly not until all of me was present. I told her that it didn't seem appropriate to me, because if I entered the room in the way she was espousing I would be teasing and joking with the children. That didn't seem at all professional to me, or very much like a doctor. Her answer was once again a question; was I afraid to discover what kind of mistakes I'd be making? From that point on the direction was clear, and I did enter the room, and I did joke, and tease, and play; and I did make plenty of mistakes. However, lo and behold, I was not only finding myself but also the more hidden and vulnerable aspects of those I was with. In learning from my mistakes, my view of others was expanding. It made me deeply appreciate words that I both heard and uttered myself, which now echoed throughout my being. Mistakes are not failures, as long as you learn from them. Play became a significant facet of how I worked, and with it my work was more rewarding. An added bonus that I hadn't anticipated, was a capacity to work in my play, which made my play much more fun.

In searching for some clinical vignettes that could bring this point out, at first I was at a loss. My playful attitude, in one form or another, is a feature with everyone I see. Occasionally it is explicit, most often woven into the fabric of everything that takes place. For example, absurdities have always struck me as funny and made me laugh, whether in myself or others. Sometimes it has taken the person I am seeing by surprise when I react this way, but it is a vital feature of my person. A moment that I identify as the time I truly became a psychoanalyst involved this element. It was my first patient who was using the couch as a part of his treatment. He felt extremely anxious about placing himself in that position; lying down and out of my sight. His initial response was to ask a flurry of questions concerning the purpose of these conditions, and what he could expect. Of course it is important to shed light on what was pushing his questions forward, which no doubt was more relevant than the particular questions themselves. However, to ignore that this individual's primary concern was wrapped up in the questions and that an answer was called for, would be both insensitive and blind to the experience this person was having. At any rate I found myself repeating words that had been etched into my mind during the course of my training as a proper response to questions. Suddenly there I was uttering the words, "What made you ask?" Hearing my voice and what I was saying sounded so absurd that i began to laugh. My patient was somewhat startled until I explained that I was laughing at myself. Under the circumstances my question was more a product of my uneasiness, perhaps matching his own. What followed was a very meaningful discussion about the significance of the couch in fostering a free associative mode, so that more hidden feelings would have a pathway to be expressed. That particular patient was quite prim and overly serious, and found my playful attitude a positive influence.

It is certainly essential to be judicious in selecting when, how, and with whom to introduce playfulness and humor, for some may need time to fully appreciate that play is always about serious matters. The decision is not easy to make, which was brought out in the treatment of a young schizophrenic woman. The dilemma that faced me was magnified by the extent of her disturbance, and her tendency to engage in what could be very destructive actions. Obviously it was an extremely serious matter, yet I knew from the start that if I maintained a serious attitude it would drive her away. On the other side encouraging playfulness was an essential ingredient if a working alliance was to be established, but this could readily encourage those harmful actions.

The intial contact was made by a family member who called in desperation, describing her as "psychotic". She was delusional, irrational, hadn't eaten, acted bizarre, and wouldn't communicate. She had been in therapy on two prior occasions and after a short time angrily refused to continue. I asked to talk to her and she was brought to the phone. After repeating to her what I had been told I asked if she would like to make an appointment. Her voice was very hostile as she stated there was no reason to do so and there was nothing wrong. I replied that it seemed like there was alot of trouble and I would give her my phone number in case she changed her mind. This made me aware that I was strongly influenced by the family member who had called and was unwittingly trying to entice her to come in. I informed her of this awareness, jokingly referring to my stupidity and thanked her for calling it to my attention. She said good night with a softer tone in her voice and hung up.

In this brief interchange a great deal was communicated. The patient displayed a surface compliance in coming to the phone, and I ultimately recognized how I had been affected by someone other than her. I also expressed a willingness to listen and be guided by her input, making my playful attitude apparent in laughing at my mistake. Implicitly respect was shown for her autonomy.

Several days later she called to ask for an appointment. Upon entering my office for the first time she immediately laid down on the couch. I expressed my surprise and she related her action to an earlier contact with a psychoanalyst. When she saw the couch she just thought that was what she was supposed to do. I laughed, recalling our contact on the phone when she had let me know very forcefully how destructive it was for her to follow someone else's direction. She also laughed, sat up, and began to tell me why she came.

Here even at this early stage her readiness to engage in the relationship was facilitated partly by my question as to why she would lie down on the couch, but I suspect it was more the light hearted tone in which I had asked it. Her laughter was quite genuine, suggesting that she was relieved by my response. The way that she had anticipated submission would be demanded indicated that something in her wanted that to be the case. By implication, however, it looked as though she also hoped that would not happen.

She then bitterly remarked that talking seemed useless to her. Her entire life had been spent analyzing her feelings and it led her nowhere. She thought of her life as made up of empty words and experiences of conformity. She constantly made lists of things to do or of places to go, but could never be spontaneous; always producing what others expected of her. Consequently she did well in school and her family was proud of her. Her mother seemed totally enveloping, like an octopus with tentacles that surrounded and squeezed the life out of her. Never did she have a feeling of making a decision of her own. With these words she recalled episodes of not eating, as if that was the only way she could be in charge of herself. This reminded her of a recent decision she had made to not move, eat, or have any bodily function. Her feeling was that any movement would put her in jeopardy of being taken over by whoever happened to be in her vicinity. She felt completely open to being invaded.

Her description vividly portrayed the depleted existence of her childhood years, along with an enormous fear of being drawn into a suffocating fusion and merger type of dependency, all with an aura of grimness. To me this meant she could readily transform anything I did into a threatening reenactment of her being engulfed and destroyed. It underscored to me the importance of my respect for, and encouragement of, her autonomy and decision making power. Also she had such an extreme reaction to serious-ness that allowing my playfulness free rein might very well sup-port a healthy and effective working alliance between us.

During the next several months she continued to stress how foolish it was to talk, yet went on to do exactly that. The empha-sis was on how mechanical she had been, could never play or feel any joy, and was always afraid of being spontaneous. Nevertheless she was successful in school and decided to go to college. She thought of it as an escape from the unbearable temptation she had to get enveloped by a relationship. She felt like two separate peo-ple living a lie. Inside it was as if there was another person search-ing for someone to love. She was thus terrified either way; that she might find someone and that she might not. She graduated from college, got a job, met an artist, and fell deeply in love. The man she loved felt like an extension of herself. He was spontaneous, playful, immature, irresponsible, and motivated solely by whim and fantasy. He was all the things she had never been but wanted to be. With him she felt exhilarated, unsure of her boundaries, confused, and at times disoriented. Soon she began to feel she was merged with everybody. Any conversation she heard entered her. She felt increasingly frightened and like she had no skin, began to hear voices and had vivid fantasies that she couldn't separate from memories. One was that she was a criminal and the police were after her. Her terror kept mounting until she finally decided that the only way to hold onto herself was to stay in one position, totally immobile, and not use any bodily function.

My dilemma was now becoming clearer. Were I to take the stance of paying exclusive attention to formulating interpretive words, in a serious manner, it had the potential of reenforcing the depleted false self so dominant during her developmental years. This would make her feel trapped, with the end result being an avoidance of the emotional attachment she needed for her growth to take place. On the other hand were I to encourage her spontaneity and expression of her fantasies it could readily activate the fusion and merger experiences that threw her into a psychotic episode. It made me realize that I would have to listen carefully to find a way to walk this precarious tightrope. My impression at this point was that it required my maintaining a spontaneous and playful attitude, while encouraging the same in her. Alone it would not be enough, for i would also have to direct all of my efforts toward bringing clarity to the meaning of her experiences. My hope was that in approaching her in this fashion she could gain a fuller understanding of herself and not have to act upon her fantasies.

I told her that she had originally started her treatment under duress and felt talking did not good. I agreed with her that talking in the way she defined it did no good and wondered why she continued to do so. She looked puzzled and wanted to know what I meant. I described meaningful lessons I had learned from dogs and infants, who used no words, and I thought this was the kind of talking she needed. She started to cry as she spoke of being caged and needing to be free. She had to fly like a bird and asked if I believed in magic. I smiled answering that I didn't think she could survive without magic, and then defined it as the capacity to be so profoundly in touch with the laws of nature that it seemed supernatural. This idea both intrigued and excited her, but she wondered if I thought she might be able to fly. I said I could feel myself wanting her to be able to fly, though my impression was that she couldn't get off of the ground.

I had understood her words as being used to defend against infantile preverbal experiences, and I was explicit encouraging this infantile mode of communication. I thought she was giving me brief glimpses of the kind of conditions she needed in order to grow. This involved supporting her regressive longings, but in a contained relationship capable of fostering her autonomy. This was how I perceived her questions about magic and flying. Were I to discourage her, she could easily perceive me as an enveloping, restrictive representative of reality. At the same time it gave me an opportunity to shine a light on the deeper meaning of her questions, while supporting her desire to fly freely. I am sure my words were delivered in a seriously playful mode, yet appreciating the terrible position she was in. The symbolic meaning of flying was directing my answer, knowing full well that this was an area of confusion in her mind. It carried with it the risk of encouraging to translate her wish into some potentially dangerous action. Yet to have curbed my spontaneous response, in order to explain its meaning, would have introduced a more distancing and somber attitude; something she did not need.

I was trying to find my way through this difficult and complex maze, with an acute awareness of her deficiencies in symbolization. She thus could readily receive what I was saying literally, leading to behavior with serious consequences. However, for me to in any way act as an extension of what for her was an annihilative external reality, could only serve to drive her away. She would then successfully avoid the attachment necessary for integration to take place. This was the attachment that could enable her to symbolically fly. She had spent her life as a slave to the wishes and expectations of others, and I heard her questions asking if I'd be able to guard her autonomy when she was in an infantile, undifferentiated state. In telling her I thought she could gain the ability to fly, I was saying she could be separate and differentiated.

She then elaborated on her increasing awareness of the cages she built inside that prevented her from having a life, as her desire to run away and fly got stronger. I indicated my support of her desire, along with my concern that she might embark on such a journey prematurely before she was ready to "spread her wings".

I was trying to reflect upon the importance of her becoming more fully engaged in the treatment as a prerequisite for achieving differentiation. In addition, I was hoping she could see the destructiveness of a defensive flight from the regression that was occurring. I was quite concerned that she would act upon this urge to fly in order to avoid the overwhelming anxiety associated with the regressive pull she felt. However, we did have a common understanding that she was in treatment to gain the strength to fly.

The "crazy" behavior, which frightened her family, she called "rattling her cage". She recognized that much of it was motivated by a powerful need to provoke her "jailers" into putting more extreme restrictions upon her. These kinds of insights were growing out of the playful ways in which all of this was expressed. She noticed that she could not control her "cage rattling". It became predominant whenever she would feel closer to me, or felt good about herself. A telephone call to me was prescribed as her medication when the impulse to rattle her cage was aroused.

At this point she revealed a secret fantasy that had kept hope alive in her. It came from a time during her childhood when she saw a portrait of an Indian woman and elaborated a fantasy of the woman as a mother who encouraged independence. With mounting intensity she described her need to fly to India to find this woman. She didn't want to fly there in her imagination, she had done that all of her life and it meant nothing. It had to be the actual experience. She then acted upon the fantasy by making numerous efforts to board an airplane, though she was stopped each time since she had no ticket. My response was to emphasize how she had the right idea, but was going about it in the wrong way and at the wrong time.

I was walking a narrow line with her trying to strengthen the part of her that was seeking a healthy interaction with a mothering figure, which was the right idea. At the same time I was gently,

jokingly, but also seriously trying to interpret the distorted direction she was drawn toward. Distorted in that it kept her from
making the very attachment she was so driven to find. I related
this to her effort to create the right conditions with me, so the
treatment would make the fantasy real. My regressive identification with her frantic attempts to hold on to her autonomy and
freedom., enabled me to empathize with her experience. The focus
of my attention was on diminishing her need to flee from the very
conditions that were required to accomplish her goal of being
independent. Of course there was the ever present danger of
encouraging her acting out. I could sense the tenuousness of our
alliance and the ease with which it could be ruptured were prohibitions or restrictions to enter my attitude.

During this period much pressure was placed upon me by her
family to meet with them. The patient made it clear that if I spoke
with them the treatment would end. The office had become a contained space for her, within which she could find herself. Were her
family to come in the door that space would be hopelessly con-
taminated. I felt she was underlining the necessity of my not being
pressured by her into behaving like someone who could not let her
go. On one occasion she announced that her family was in the
waiting room. She wanted me to inform them that I wouldn't
speak with them. I laughed, commenting that she seemed to be
inviting me to make her therapy impossible, since i would then be
talking with them. She smiled, later referring to this moment as
crucial. It was like a breath of fresh air to have what was said be
what was done.

Shortly thereafter I received a phone call from another country.
She had gotten on a plane, was being held, and refused to explain
anything. The only identification she had was my bill. She was put
on the phone and I laughingly stated, "Well, you are two-thirds
cured". She giggled, explaining that she had gone to the airport to

fly to India. She made herself "invisible", had gotten as far as another country, but was stopped for not having a passport. Feeling totally defeated, she just wanted to kill herself. She could feel herself falling apart as she was being questioned. It occurred to her that if she told the truth they would consider her insane, but if she told a lie they would understand and send her home. She decided at that moment to remain silent. When she heard my voice she anticipated either an attack or some kind of condescending comment. Hearing my laugh gave her an infusion of life and energy, she told the truth, and returned home.

In the succeeding sessions she spoke of her involvement with acting upon a fantasy that she needed in order to live. She saw how it protected her from forming a deeper attachment to me. She was searching for a mother in India that was there to find in her treatment. It was clear to her now that she had been trying to heal herself, but had run away from the relationship in which that potential existed. Most important was her need to discover that I could allow her the autonomy, independence, and freedom to move. Her flight was a prelude to her entering the relationship with that degree of trust.

After she returned she couldn't sleep, eat, or remove her contact lenses. She couldn't sleep because she was terrified of being totally enveloped by the powerful forces within. This expressed her fear of the regression that was now extremely active. She described being awake as a way of staying alive, facing herself, and not escaping. She thought of sleeping as being enveloped, escaping and running away. I laughed, answering that it seemed to me she had it all backwards. Sleeping to me seemed like the equivalent of flying; of entering her internal world without the weight of her defenses. Staying awake looked like an escape, reflecting her opposition to these infantile experiences. She was also terrified that if she ate she would gorge herself and never be able to stop.

The only way to manage was to not eat, or to eat only the barest minimum. She feared being near people, as she experienced her appetite coming to life. In addition, she feared she would become blind if she removed her contact lenses. She could see clearly with them on, but without them her vision would become blurry. Once again I told her she had the right idea, but was going about it in the wrong way. She did need to see clearly and was frightened that her vision would become undifferentiated. Her response to my consistently pointing out these reversals, and especially my joking, playful manner in doing so, was to begin to expose herself to food. This gave her a feeling of regulation and restraint. She selected food to prepare in interesting and imaginative ways. Skills and abilities that had always been dormant now were accessible. Along with it she allowed herself to sleep, and dreams were readily retained. She reported a dream in which she was in the court of a French king and was offerred anything she desired. However, she was unable to permit herself to have anything. The dream made it apparent to her that the obstacles were within herself, which was enormously relieving. It made her feel in charge of her life for the first time. My first name and the French word for king were identical, a fact that she couldn't help but notice.

Treatment was opening potentials and making her aware of the significance of words. They could now be used to articulate her feelings and experiences, aiding her in gaining perspective. This was a marvelous feeling for her, as she recalled what it was like to have no skin. She could feel like a whole person with conflicts, feelings, and problems. A key factor centered around the meaning of flying. She stated she had to fly in order to live and I agreed. To both of us, flying meant to be able to move freely. In my view it signified facilitating a regression, which would entail a temporary loss of more advanced psychic functions until a new integration was attained. At that point she would be free to fly. For her she could only anticipate being enveloped. She feared I'd be unable to aid her in the task of self differentiation, and she would lose the ability to fly.

My playful attitude certainly played a role in encouraging her into the dramatic enactment of a flight, which did express her wish to be a separate individual. It also gave her the experience of feeling my appreciation for the importance of her action. In this sense I think the acting out was probably necessary. There was much to suggest that if I had not been able to ally myself with the meaning of her fantasy that she would have been unable to fully engage in the attachment she required. In one way acting on the fantasy carried her away from the treatment, but the connection was strengthened by my recognition of its significance to her. My playfulness in accepting it permitted her to return fully prepared to focus upon her infantile strivings. Had I been unwilling to appreciate the positive elements in her risky behavior, it might well have undermined her sense of trust. This situation showed the powerful influence of a genuine and spontaneous playful attitude in dealing with an extremely serious matter.

The root meaning of the word humor refers to the fluids that sustain life. Its extension into playfulness is a vital aspect in enabling the internalization of serious words designed to heal psychological wounds. Often serious discussions can become so heavy that the messages they carry get lost. A playful approach expands the room to absorb their meaning more easily. Many more powerful emotions can be held and seen more clearly when the atmosphere they emerge in does not have to be reacted against.

Some years ago I needed a reminder of the importance of keeping playfulness vibrant and alive, when I could feel myself becoming much too serious about the events taking place in my life. I was listening to the radio as I prepared to go to work searching for the source of the heaviness I felt. At just that moment a march was being played and I realized the date was March 4th. It was then that my special holiday—Parade Day—was born. This would be the day that would remind me of the essential task of holding my playful nature close, so its value would always be appreciated. In doing so my entire mood and outlook lightened. From that moment on every March 4th I march forth to a tune in my head. The reminder resonates throughout my entire being. Characteristically on that day I march into my office from the parking lot with a smile on my face, feeling somewhat silly, playful, and glad to be reminded. One day I was doing just that when I could feel eyes on me, and looked up to see a group of construction workers watching what must have seemed like very peculiar behavior. To have stopped would have made it worse, so I just kept right on marching. I smiled as I thought of how foolish I must have looked, and was pleased that my playfulness was so strongly present. So it is that I keep marching on, keeping the essence of play viable within me where it enriches and enhances whatever I may be.

Chapter 14

A String of Pearls (odds and ends)

W isdom is defined as the ability to discriminate between what is true and what is false. In this final chapter I would like to string together a number of seemingly unrelated ideas, insights, beliefs, and judgements, which I think of as containing wisdom. Taken together they reflect upon things I knew as a child but did not have words for. Compiling the list made me aware of a theme running through all of the items. They concern lessons I've learned over the years, which I believe in deeply, that appear to run counter to what many colleagues would follow or to what I have been taught in various educational settings. It captures my impression that there are powerful cultural forces that act in opposition to, rather, than support of, a given individual person's opportunities for growth. I don't find that surprising, for to follow a pathway of truth is an extremely difficult task; though vastly rewarding in the long run. Lies, by way of contrast, provide a quick answer and can easily foster illusions of safety. Furthermore, everybody lies in one way or another, either openly or hidden even from themselves. It is part of the human condition.

Exposing the lies we tell to ourselves can be, and usually is, a life-long process, opening up doors to the full range of potentials for richness and vitality that each person possesses.

In their own way deliberate lies I consider to be wonderful. First of all the person is awareof the lie, and perhaps at least some of the motive for it. More importantly, however, in listening carefully it is often possible to hear a deeper truth contained within the lie; much in the manner of a halloween costume. The person is selecting a costume specifically designed to hide who they are, but what has been chosen frequently reveals a more hidden truth.

Lies are to the truth what cravings are to the appetite; and the two are often confused one with the other. Physical appetite emerges from the center of a person, seeking the proper nourishment for one's body to be healthy and function well. All other aspects of what is desired are spinoffs or reflections of this center. The same principle is at work in regard to the effect of the truth upon a person's emotional life. For a person to experience their full potential, appetite must be the guide, just as the truth must lead in emotional matters.

Many people simply do not know what they want to do, how to go about finding it, or of not having a clear idea of what is important to them. These are all symptomatic of having "lost one's appetite". The hunger, however, to be directed towards something can be so strong that cravings will be latched onto as a substitue for the loss. It is exactly the way that lies carry with them the illusion that a person has in fact achieved what they have wanted most. Again it shouts out that one's appetite is missing.

Any steps towards finding answers to these difficult questions must begin with being able to differentiate between appetite and cravings, since cravings are an attempt to compensate for the loss of appetite. The difference is not all that difficult to discern, though there may be some grey areas. Appetite can generally wait to be met, provided the wait is not too long; whereas cravings have an urgency to them demanding that they be satisfied immediately if not sooner. Appetite is thoughtful and discriminating, craving lives off of adrenaline-like experiences or their equivalent in rapidly metabolized foods In one sense it might appear to be a paradox (though clearly it is not) that individuals who are grossly overweight could be said to have lost their appetite.

The significance of speaking the truth arises on innumerable occasions in the course of a person's life. Easy to say, but difficult to do, for a whole host of reasons. One vital one is that the person may not always know fully what the truth consists of in order to be able to speak it. It would be much more accurate to say that it is important to speak as much of the truth as is known. Approaching any situation in this manner has consequences and depending upon how these are viewed they can be seen as good, bad, helpful, or harmful. On many occasions I have seen that speaking the truth will destroy a weak relationship, but it also will strengthen a strong one. I think most people intuitively know it, yet find it threatening to discover and avoid putting it to the test. It can be quite a dilemma to risk seeking in which direction it will travel. That is; until one considers an additional factor. The truth hurts, as the saying goes, of which there is no doubt. However, lies damage. The implication is that it's bad for someone to hurt. With the exception of those times when the truth is used as a weapon (in which case it is hard to think of it as the truth), the hurt that may result gives the injured party an opportunity to learn. Whether they do or don't take advantage of it is entirely out of one's control.

There is so much to learn in so many different areas of life that it is no wonder so much confusion exists. I notice it a lot whenever the subject of limits and limitations is raised, particularly if those words are used interchangeably. Although what they refer to is related, there is a significant difference in the phenomena they are meant to explain. To reach one's limits is an exciting event, and experienced as such, for limits define the fulfilling of potentials. On the other hand limitations are frustrating and painful; they define what is possible but not realized (for whatever reason). It is in this arena that the light and dark side of envy come into play. The light side of envy is a pleasure and appears as admiration for others who exhibit capacities consonant with one's potentials. The dark side of envy is an awful load to carry. It mobilizes one to behave destructively towards anyone displaying these qualities, thereby compromising the ability to grow, or interrupting and interfering with any opportunity to realize those very potentials.

Somewhere in the course of almost everyday I will hear someone comment about a committed relationship. What is surprising to me is how frequently it is simply taken for granted that to be committed is a positive quality. I shake my head in disbelief. The word committed is most often used in regard to jails and mental hospitals where it is quite appropriate. In a human relationship to be tied down in this fashion, it seems to me, does not leave much room for anyone to grow. There is something off base when such an attachment is seen as a desirable goal. Having duty and obligation assume this kind of priority, so as to rule a relationship, would have to limit the freedom of both parties. The concern about eliminating commitment as a necessary component of an intimate tie centers around the idea that freedom would only result in infidelity. Unfortunately the idea that commitment strengthens intimacy is clung to, despite all the evidence pointing to the fallacy of this belief. Maintaining this illusion can offer some sense of security, false though it may be, and with it ease the anxiety one or both parties may harbor that they will be abandoned or betrayed. In truth the less committed one is, and the more involved in developing and nourishing a foundation of friendship, the more that intimacy is enhanced. Sexuality is then a major avenue for strengthening the bonds of the relationship. The need to seek addictive forms of sexuality elsewhere is thereby not a factor. A foundation of friendship is characterized by the welcoming of spontaneity, along with a deep appreciation of the value of speaking the truth. The confident knowledge of this attribute enables the relationship to encourage what is best and constructive for both, while providing a setting in which any problem can be worked out. It is not based upon committment, but upon integrity, compassion, and a common devotion to finding clarity.

There was a time when I considered promises to be sacrosanct. I thought I was doing something admirable in making a promise and even better in keeping it. Over the years I have come to look at it in quite a different manner. I now realize that when I promise something I am insuring that nothing either can or will change. Originally I had thought of it as a positive message, in that I was giving some sense of security. However, over time the falseness of that reassurance has become apparent to me. Wordlessly, I think everyone intuitively knows it. I have come to appreciate how much more reassuring it is to have confidence that an honest response will be given, rather than a promise. There is then the space and opportunity to complain, be angry, disappointed, or hurt with the firm knowledge that to speak openly and genuinely will deepen and strengthen the relationship. There is then an option available to both sides, at any point, to change their mind. Change can be welcome, with the only concern being as to whether it is for the best.

I have yet to meet a child who is ever reassured by being told they are good. The reasons are no mystery, for all children are bad sometimes and often it's fun. What is necessary is not so much telling them how good they are, but in knowing how to help them with their feelings about being bad. The door is opened to what can be very meaningful discussions as to what is good and what is bad. In its extremes it is usually easy to determine, but there are interesting grey areas where it is not so clear. Identifying these uncertainties, with all of their ambiquities, can expand the minds of all concerned.

When I am asked a question about the appropriateness of spanking children , my immediate answer "only if you lose control"almost always draws a quizical look. It is as if my words are heardas advocating the loss of control in spanking a child. What I mean is that the only way I can make any sense of a reason for spanking a child is if someone has lost control. It is certainly in no way desirable, but I can see nothing sensible about dealing with a child that way. It gives a powerful, destructive message that bullying and even violence is an answer to what can be difficult problems, bypassing the many options that could facilitate learning. It probably is a reflection of the confusion between discipline and control. Discipline means to follow the teachings of someone you admire, something every child needs. Control means to prohibit, restrain, and intimidate, something as far as I can see nobody needs. One leads to internal regulation, which is necessary to have a full life; the other to stopping out of fear of retribution, which does little towards solving anything.

It is quite striking to me to observe how frequently the idea of being held accountable for one's behavior has become an exercise in finger pointing and blame. I believe it is vital to be held accountable, especially to one's self as well as to others. It carries with it an opportunity to incorporate every facet of one's being, including those that have been rendered inaccessible. All too often, however, a person has been so inundated with shame—invoking or punitive responses (for not doing their part or for behaving badly in someone's eyes), that to even raise the question of their role in some experience is taken as a rebuke. Taking full responsibility for one's actions is a golden gate, opening up a chance to gain a more complete knowledge of oneself and with it retrieve what has been lost. Taking responsibility points a direction towards learning with compassion instead of a way of assigning blame.

Part of the trouble comes from confusion around what is, and what is not, responsible behavior. Until there is clarity in this area conformity will take precedence over what is constructive and growth promoting. There is no question that in raising children it is important to help them take responsibility for themselves. However, it is not always easy to determine what that entails. The struggle to identify what is being responsible is a vital one to engage in, so that rigid rules are not substituted for sensitive decision making. Such an act in itself is responsible behavior on the part of a parent, a good start towards finding answers. A common situation illustrating the nature of the problem is captured when a child is given a homework assignment. To begin with the assignment could be an exercise in repetition given as a substitue for inadequate teaching. In that case were a child to make the choice of doing the assignment, instead of going out to play where there are many opportunities for learning and growth, it would be irresponsible. Yet it is quite common for it to be presented the other way around, as if it was responsible to conform to an irresponsible demand. It is then usually justified by the "rational-lies" given that one must adapt to the real world. On the other side, however, were the homework to be a genuine spur to growth and learning and the child chose playing to avoid it, that would be an irresponsible act. Much can be discovered by facing these matters with an open mind, not just assuming that adults are always correct in their assessments. The implication is that if children are left to their own devices they will always be irresponsible.

It looks to me like people can become so preoccupied with what they consider to be a desired outcome that they may do, or condone doing anything, to achieve it. When these kinds of efforts lead nowhere there is little thought given to whether it is on the wrong track, but only wondering how to do the same thing more forcefully. What is even worse is when the goal is achieved, and in the process of doing so all belief systems are cast aside, as if the end result was all that mattered. Under these conditions the consequence is often reflected in the initial goal losing its appeal. What may then go unrecognized is that the steps taken so eroded the foundation of integrity, so necessary to give meaning to life, that what was reached cannot be enjoyed. In shorthand this phenomenon is called selling your soul to the devil.

It can take a long time to fully appreciate how the means are truly everything, whereas the ends take care of themselves. Each step taken is then guided by what is true, straightforward, and right, giving no thought to an outcome, and thereby leads to another step guided by the same principle. Eventually an outcome evolves, but the person has been true to themselves all along that pathway. Basically the outcome is incidental for the journey has been deeply valued. There are innumerable incidents throughout history wherein the ends have been used to justify usually very destructive means. Although in some instances it may appear as though a positive result has taken place, it is generally temporary. In the long run the erosive effect of this approach becomes apparent.

Any given incident can be examined with this principle in mind. In doing so it will become evident as to how easy it is to slide into this position. However the exploration provides a way to get back on track. It reminds me of the many times I have been told that it would be so simple to momentarily abandon this cherished principle, and in doing so achieve the necessary wherewithal to realize what would otherwise be impossible. Then I could return to what I believed. My response that in abandoning what I valued I would be putting the end ahead of the means, and in doing so the whole experience would become meaningless, was received with a look of puzzlement. Yet it was not difficult to see that you cannot travel from St. Louis to Los Angeles and Boston Simultaneously. Pure and simple it means traveling in opposite directions, which lead to different places. A difficult concept to grasp, but a vital one to follow.

Work, play, love, and the activities that sustain them is one way of categorizing all of life's experiences. Sustaining activities are those that provide, support, and enhance necessary adaptations to the shifting conditions of an unpredictable outside world. They include self care, exercise of responsibility, money management, awareness of time and space, all behavior designed to find opportunities, and anything else required to manage a meaningful life. These activities can be experienced in a host of ways ranging from invigorating, challenging and fulfilling to depleting, demanding, and a source of resentment. One indication of stress, and a first sign of psychological difficulty, is when these activities are experienced as drudgery.

Many people refer to their work as drudgery, and so it may be. However, it may be due to thinking of their means of making a livlihood as their work, when it is a self sustaining activity. Work may sometimes be a hobby, defined as play, or something not as yet discovered. Work involves the use of a person's unique talents and skills, guided by their ambitions and goals, on the background of their particular morals and standards. By this definition work cannot be drudgery. The way a person makes a living, however, can. Nevertheless when it is seen as a way of facilitating work (as well as love and play) it is no longer drudgery. At its worst it is then simply something that must be done. It is a fortunate person, indeed, whose work and means of making a living are one and the same.

Self attacks can encompass a range of experiences. Those that are relatively mild, generally referred to as self pity or feeling sorry for yourself, may offer some moments of respite from the difficult task of learning and growing. This kind of rest is needed at times and, as long as it is not taken seriously, may be helpful. Other forms are more intense and as far as I can tell serve no useful purpose. Feeling bad, or guilty, about some hurtful action is quite different than a self attack. Guilt can be a catalyst in the process of learning that leads to correcting mistakes. However, it is easy for a person to move from feeling bad into a self attack, in which case nothing constructive occurs.

It took me a long time to discover that self attacks are most debilitating because they obscure vision. Feeling bad, or guilty, can help a person to identify aspects of themselves that have become twisted and destructive, thereby aiding in the attainment of greater clarity. Sometimes the purpose of a self attack may be precisely to destroy that possibility; for the end result is that the truth remains hidden. Herein lies the distinction; there is no searching, there is no exploring; there is no curiosity, only a scathing denunciation.

This kind of attitude may readily develop in people with a variety of disabilities, for it can be easy to hide behind the obvious problems the disability creates. In that way such a person becomes an invalid, and may even refer to themselves with that term. To be an invalid signifies that what you are showing is not valid, as would be the case if the disability is used in that fashion.

It is easy to forget that all internal thought and language is based upon symbols. Everyone dreams and is acquainted with the "strangeness" of symbolic imagery. The quality of these symbols is such that many believe their primary purpose is to disguise internal meaning. Although there are times when it may have that purpose, I think another feature of symbols is too often overlooked. This has to do with their being a primitive form of communication, and as such they can be viewed as a different language.

In adults internal thought and language have become so depersonified that the imagery upon which it is based is not immediately available. Children are much closer to that process, though their capacity to articulate what the particular symbols mean to them is less developed. Adding to the difficulty is that people speaking the same language unwittingly assume that the words they use have the same meaning. In fact it may be quite different. Just as certain symbols may have universal meaning, for they have to possess the quality of whatever is being symbolized, it is only through knowing the unique meaning to a given individual that what they are designed to express can be fully understood. The same is also true of the depersonified symbols of spoken language. This would be unmistakeable and clearly apparent if the two parties were speaking two separate languages to each other. Keeping this in mind we can then be more curious as to what is actually being said, rather than taking it for granted that we know. It is no mystery that when words like right, wrong, good, bad, etc. are used, they may have a completely different meaning to each.

In this context I don't know is a wonderful answer to a question. First and foremost what it means must be understood. Does it mean it's none of your business?, does it mean I don't want to think or talk about it?, or literally that the person does not know. The answer serves to eliminate all the other possibilites leaving the field open for knowledge to emerge and communication to be better understood.

This problem is also present in regard to yeses and no's. It can be extremely difficult to distinguish what they actually mean. No must come before yes. The so-called terrible two's refers to an age when a child is likely to say no to everything, in order to discover if it is truly safe to express what is meant. Once a child knows that he or she is entitled to say no, a genuine yes can be given. Too often yes is based upon conformity and no on rebelliousness.

Certain sayings have stuck in my mind, because the messages they contain express a cherished value or belief succinctly. They stand as sign posts to remind me of what is important, especially at moments when I may inadvertently stray or be blinded.

The first refers to the profession I have chosen as my work, feeling blessed since it is also how I make a living. The saying captures my having been drawn to it as a choice because it required a kind of honesty I aspired to reach, was a field too vast to be mastered in a lifetime with so much to learn, and the rewards must evolve from what I come to understand and not depend upon the gratitude of others. The saying is;

"We the willing, led by the unknown, are doing the
impossible, for the ungrateful".
Another I have only recently come across, although its message has been with me for a long time. It has to do with how
elusive feelings can be if you chase after their meaning only
directed by your efforts, will, and intellectual processes. The
most effective way to see into this deeper realm of the mind is to
eliminate outside distractions and be still, with a receptive attitude toward whatever arises. With such a stance it will reach
you. The saying is;
"Don't just do something, stand there".
What could easily be called a paradox and has always interested me, is how much credibility is given to things that can be
seen whereas things that are invisible elicit doubt, uncertainty, and
disbelief. This is in spite of the awareness that so much of what we
value is invisible to the eye and only visible to the heart. This is the
place where belief resides. The saying is;
"Believing is seeing".
An openness to new learning is always a valuable position to
take, and in that context I would like to be fully alert whenever
the time comes for me to die. At least I will have a chance to face
what is unquestionably unknown. I once overheard two children
discussing adults, and categorizing them as grown-ups or grow-
ing- ups. One referring to people who were closed in that they
knew all the answers and had a rule to follow for everything. The
other to people who were open and listened to a child's contribution. It had absolutely nothing to do with their chronological age.
The saying is;
"If its green it grows, if its ripe it rots".
I have also believed that a person's chronological age was not
the determining factor as to what they could or could not do. That
had to be determined by what they were capable of doing at any

given time. The world addresses this differently for a host of reasons, but the saying is;

"What age would you be if you didn't know what you was?"

This has to do with what many people have discovered. The more one comes to learn and know about any given topic, the wider one's field of ignorance grows. Furthermore this important realization establishes the groundwork for learning to continue and thus must be a source of comfort not anxiety. The saying is;

"It takes a long time to know nothing".

Finally some brief comments about some features in the way I conduct my practice that will of necessity vary from one person to an other. It is essential that whatever decisions are made be genuine and true, regardless of what that entails. Above all a healer must be guided by that principle.

In my opinion the establishment of a proper fee is a vital part of the treatment and if the fee is not right the treatment can't be right. This means it has to be right for me as well as my patient, for were I to sacrifice myself it would not be good for me or for anyone I work with. Thus I have no set fee, beyond an amount above which I will not accept. This feels right to me. It is impossible for the same fee to be right for everyone I would see, and the occasion has arisen where I simply could not afford what was right for a potential patient. In that case it is best for me not to work with that person and try to help them find a place where it is possible.

When I go on vacation I always leave a number where I can be reached, and anyone I see will know they are free to call at anytime. I welcome the calls, because it has never made sense to me to have someone take over for me when I am away. It takes me so long to get to know someone well enough to have a sense of what is in their best interest, that it is hard for me to picture how someone could come in cold, even being informed by me, and handle something no matter how much of an emergency. It seems unfair to the patient. However, I could not take such a position if I was not comfortable in saying no. If, for whatever reason, I don't feel able to talk or am otherwise occupied it is important that I inform the caller and set up a time when I can. In that regard the term generally used for taking over this function is "covering" for someone, which sounds quite accurate. I do not want to have anyone cover anything, if there is something that needs to be said I prefer to have it said by me and directly in person. If the phone calls are exploitative or destructive and my accepting a call encourages it, what better way to have it out in the open to be discovered than to have the pathway open. If I am blind to it, I certainly am not as likely to see it with the pathway closed.

I also accept phone calls at anytime, day or night, and I understand that if they weren't genuinely welcome that option should not be encouraged or provided. Again that would be a disservice. I do not consider it an imposition, for I believe there are those who really need such an avenue. In addition I do not mind being awakened, for I love the process of going to sleep and it gives me another chance to do it again.

I occasionally use medication as an adjunct to the treatment, but like everything else it is determined by the patient. There is always a place for allies in the process of healing and medicine can at times be precisely what is needed. The determination has to be made as to whether the substance being used facilitates the ability to contain greater intensities of feeling or whether it numbs or puts them to sleep. In the latter instance it would be a drug, in which case it would be far from being an ally. I frequently hear the term non-compliance used to refer to a patient's refusal to comply with the doctor's orders, particularly in regard to medication. The implication is that the patient is somehow doing something bad, which in my opinion is remarkably insensitive as well as blind. I should hope that a person would refuse to comply with someone's orders. A doctor is always making decisions concerning what is indicated for a given patient on the basis of what that person's body or mind is calling out for. In physical terms the patient's body is informing the doctor as to what is needed, sometimes abetted by tests designed to increase what can be told. It is no different with emotional factors. The doctor's task is to not only provide what is possible, but also help the patient see where and how the choice was made. Therefore if the patient is not following these directives it can be due to an inadequate understanding of where they came from, suggesting either more or better explanations are required; or it could mean there is something wrong with the directive, in which case a better answer can be sought. Either way it has nothing to do with compliance. I fail to see how complying can be a positive experience.

In conclusion my emphasis throughout this book has been on the nurturing, growth-promoting, and constructive influences that the truth possesses. I have also tried to bring out how essential it is for a therapist to be constantly alert to the part he or she assumes in taking the lead in unearthing what is genuine and true. Everyone lies, that is to be expected. However, a patient is entitled to lie and in fact is encouraged to do so, for it is in this way that lies can be brought into the light of day and exposed to the healing power of the truth. On the other hand the search for the truth must begin with the therapist, otherwise the search becomes a sham. In this process of discovery both parties benefit and a remarkable characteristic of the truth emerges. It is something I think everyone knows intuitively, even though many may protest initially. Put into a simple statement it would be "99% equals zero". You are either telling the truth fully and completely or it is a lie. The fact that a lie is spoken is not necessarily a problem; it is the refusal to search that is.

www.ingramcontent.com/pod-product-compliance
Lightning Source LLC
Chambersburg PA
CBHW061351280526
45784CB00001B/222